Horace M. Hale

Education in Colorado, 1861-1885

a brief history of the early educational interests of Colorado, together with

the history of the State Teachers' Association

Horace M. Hale

Education in Colorado, 1861-1885
a brief history of the early educational interests of Colorado, together with the history of the State Teachers' Association

ISBN/EAN: 9783337187972

Printed in Europe, USA, Canada, Australia, Japan

Cover: Foto ©Paul-Georg Meister /pixelio.de

More available books at **www.hansebooks.com**

1861–1885.

Education in Colorado.

A Brief History of the Early Educational Interests of Colorado, Together with the History of the State Teachers' Association, and Short Sketches of Private and Denominational Institutions.

Compiled by Order of the State Teachers' Association.

DENVER, COLO.
NEWS PRINTING COMPANY
1885.

PREFACE.

At the eleventh session of the Colorado State Teachers' Association, held at Denver, December 29, 30, and 31, 1884, among the resolutions adopted was the following:

Resolved, That the Hon. H. M. Hale, with two others whom he may appoint, shall constitute a committee, the duty of which shall be to prepare and print a pamphlet embodying the history of the schools of Colorado, and especially a history of this Association now just completing the tenth year of its life.

In pursuance of the above, Superintendent Aaron Gove, of the public schools of District No. 1, Arapahoe County, and Hon. Joseph C. Shattuck, late State Superintendent of Public Instruction, were called to aid in the work proposed.

The committee thus formed deemed it advisable to preface the history of the schools and of the Association with a summary of the history of the early settlement of the State, sufficient, at least, to form an introduction.

The fact that Colorado has just fairly completed the first quarter of a century of her existence, under the present *regime*, makes the publication of this volume seem especially opportune and desirable, to the end that future generations may have the essential facts relating to the early schools, and these compiled by living participants.

In performing the work assigned them, the committee have not striven to be exhaustive; on the contrary, the endeavor has been to be as concise as would be consistent with the end sought.

Their work is respectfully submitted with the hope that it will meet the approval of the Association and of the friends of popular education throughout the State.

HORACE M. HALE,
AARON GOVE,
JOSEPH C. SHATTUCK,
Committee.

Part I.

History of Early Educational Interests of Colorado.

Early Educational Interests.

CHAPTER I.

A LITTLE GENERAL HISTORY.

Prior to the year of our Lord 1859 little was known, by civilized America, of the region now embraced by the boundaries of Colorado. That there existed, between the then Western boundary of civilization and the Rocky Mountains, a vast, unsettled and almost unexplored country belonging to the United States, was generally understood. It was known that, while under the administration of Thomas Jefferson, in 1803, the Government purchased from France, for $15,000,000, an immense area of almost unknown land; also that later, in 1848, it had acquired by treaty with Mexico, territory to the southwest which, if less extensive than the Louisiana purchase, was equally valueless. A very large portion of the country here referred to was, as late as 1840, described in the school atlases of the day, and was known, as "The Great American Desert."

Soon after the purchase of the French territory, the United States Government sent Zebulon Pike (1806), with a few soldiers, to explore what is now a part of Colorado, and later (1819) Colonel S. H. Long on a similar mission farther north. Still later (1832) the American Fur Company sent Captain Bonneville. In 1842 and 1844 John C. Fremont, under the auspices of the Government, passed through this region *en route* to the South Pass and Oregon. Besides these expeditions, a few fur traders visited the Rocky Mountain region and established forts or trading posts on the Arkansas and Platte Rivers. Even prior to the Mexican war, quite an active trade was carried on, by means of caravans, between the Western limits of American civilization and Santa Fe—the outpost and trade center of Northern Mexico.

Previous to 1846, the Mexican Government had donated to Colorado Vigil and St. Vrain, an extensive grant of land lying south of the Arkansas River, known as the "Las Animas Land Grant." Colonel Bent had established a trading post on the Arkansas, which served as a place of refuge and defense in after years against the Indians. A few Mexicans had, prior to 1858, settled near the southern boundary of Colorado, on the Las Animas River, and a colony of fifty or more formed the settlement of Conejos, where a Jesuit Mission School was established. With the exception of the early Government explorers, the fur traders, trainmen, California emigrants, Mexicans, and perhaps a few Mormons—not forgetting the ancient Aztecs, whose records are still to be read in the Cliff Houses of the southwestern counties—Colorado had received very little civilizing influence prior to the date of what may properly be called its present civilization, or the advent of Green Russell's party of Georgians in June, 1858.

The acquisition of California from Mexico, followed almost immediately, as it was, by the discovery of gold there, led to its marvelously rapid settlement by Americans, and also to more extended explorations for the precious metals in other portions of the newly acquired territory; not such superficial, horseback explorations as history informs us were made by Vasquez Coroando, in 1540, but such as had proved remunerative to intelligent, practical miners in California.

As above stated, Green Russell's party made their advent in June, 1858. They had acquired a mining experience in their native State and in California. They prospected quite carefully all the tributaries of the Platte, and found gold, in small quantities, almost everywhere; their best results were obtained about six miles above Denver, in a dry gulch, which they christened "Montana Diggings." Finding sufficient evidence there to justify them in believing that better might be found elsewhere, they returned to the Missouri River for supplies, carrying the proof of their discoveries.

In the spring of 1859, there was a great rush to the new El Dorado. Exaggerated reports of the wonderful gold deposits that had been discovered by the Russell party in the "Pike's Peak" region had spread over the country, as such reports usually spread. Adventurers rushed in by hundreds, only to become disgusted and to turn again their faces Eastward, without even unloading their wagons, stubbornly refusing to sell, at extravagant prices, their surplus provisions to those whom they accused of encouraging the fraud. The greater portion, however, of these pioneers, in some instances from necessity, and in some from choice, remained to make more extended researches. Nearly all were inexperienced in gold hunting; many could not tell gold when they saw it. The following extract from "Fossett's Colorado" graphically portrays the peculiarities of the vanguard of Colorado's civilization:

"With the spring and summer of 1859, came a stampede Westward to the land of promise, such as has never been equalled, except in the case of California. Over the broad expanse of six hundred miles of plains, passed an almost continuous stream of humanity. The talismanic legend "gold" had created a fever and enthusiasm that no distance or hardships could repress, no danger or difficulty dispel; and so all routes over this ocean of dust and solitude were lined with caravans, and with pilgrims weary and footsore, but ever hopeful of the land and future before them. That many were doomed to disappointment is told in the unwritten history of this as well as of all other mining excitements. The roving, advanturous spirits that formed the vanguard in the settlement of Colorado came largely from the better and more enterprising classes of the East, West and South. There was a smattering of good, bad, and indifferent characters, all equally desirous of bettering their fortunes, which in many cases could not have been worse. Probably over fifty thousand men aided, in this eventful year, to enlarge that 'Western trail of immigration, which bursts into States and empires as it moves.'

"The wide awake speculator, the broken-down merchant, the farmer, mechanic, gambler, or the wanderer from foreign lands, the cultivated and the illiterate, all combined to swell the human tide that was setting in so strongly for the new land of gold out toward the setting sun. While many were admirably adapted to settle and reclaim a wilderness, large numbers soon became discouraged, and returned whence they came; but this could not arrest the progress of the oncoming multitude that followed. Probably nineteen twentieths of those goldseekers were as ignorant and inexperienced as regards mining as they well could be, and had but a faint idea of the work to be done or the hardships to be undergone in this wild rush for wealth."

After discovering gold in small quantities on South Boulder and South Clear Creek, near Idaho Springs, in 1859, followed by the grand discovery of the "Gregory Diggings" made by John H. Gregory, an experienced California miner, near the present sites of Central City and Black Hawk, in Gilpin County, matters assumed an aspect of permanence, and those who came to look resolved to stay; before the close of the year an effort was made to form a Territorial Government; some enthusiast declared for a State Government at once, deeming it unnecessary to pass through the intermediate stage of a Territory. They even went so far as to submit to the people a State constitution; this was voted down by a very large majority.

An attempt was then made to organize a Territory to be known as "Jefferson," and a delegate was sent to Congress to urge its recognition; this project failing, the people were forced to be content with asking for a recognition in the Kansas Legislature. In this they were so far successful as to induce the Legislature to form the County of Arapahoe, embracing all the western part of Kansas and extending to the Snowy Range. "Arapahoe County, Kansas," was the region styled until 1861.

Lode mining began to supplement gulch mining. The famous Bob-Tail and Gregory lodes were large producers, and Gilpin County was found to be a complete gridiron of veins, each of which was believed, by its owner, to be a reservoir of limitless wealth. One hundred linear feet on a lode was deemed sufficient to make a Croesus of its owner; therefore the miners decreed that that should be the extent of a claim; the discoverer, however, might locate two such claims.

The more prosperous camps soon became over-crowded, and when the fact became patent that every claim was not a bonanza, parties gradually drifted into unexplored regions, so that, in due time, miner's cabins and tents, and sluice boxes and windlasses were to be seen on nearly every stream in the mountains. Towns sprang into existence in a day, and in some instances were as quickly abandoned. The miners themselves were the makers, expounders, and executors of the local laws; no higher authority was sought or recognized. Here was a perfect, practical illustration of a pure democracy. Whenever an exigency arose, the people assembled and made the laws *viva voce*, and not unfrequently executed them with as little formality; yet "vice did not prevail," nor did "impious men bear sway." Thus it was, until February 26, 1861, when, Kansas having been admitted into the Union, Congress organized the Territory of Colorado, covering the same area as now, and limited by the thirty-seventh and forty-first parallels of north latitude, and the one hundred and second and one hundred and ninth meridians of west longitude. William Gilpin was sent as governor; a census taken showed a population of 25,329—4,484 of whom were women, with a sufficient number of children to at least suggest the approaching need of schools. Denver, being the *entrepot* for immigrants, and the outfitting post for miners and prospectors, had become a city of no mean proportions; brick buildings had taken the places of tents and temporary shanties; large business houses had been established, and even a mint—where gold was coined—by Clark, Gruber & Co. Not less than three banks were loaning money at from 5 to 20 per cent. per month, and yet there was no urgent demand for a school.

We have thus briefly presented the story of Colorado's infancy, not so much with the view of giving its history, as of furnishing a foundation upon which to base the chief purpose of this volume; viz., its school history and the history of the State Teachers' Association.

CHAPTER II.

HISTORY OF THE SCHOOLS.

Among the acts passed by the First Legislative Assembly of Colorado, held at Denver, in 1861, was a very comprehensive school law, similar in its provisions to that then in force in the State of Illinois. This law provided for the appointment, by the Governor, during that session, of a "Territorial Superintendent of Common Schools," who was to enter upon the duties of his office on the first day of December, 1861, and to continue until his successor was duly appointed and qualified; he was to receive an annual salary of $500. The duties were minutely prescribed and were similar to those now imposed on the State Superintendent of Public Instruction, with the additional duty of recommending to the several school districts a uniform series of text books, to be used in the schools thereof. As a matter of course, the Superintendent could accomplish little. The impulses of the people were in the right direction, but the essential elements of success—children—were wanting. Some of the first school districts organized were as large as States, while the school population numbered less than a score.

The law provided for the election, biennially, of a County Superintendent in each County, and in its general features was not essentially different from that of the present.

At the second session of the Legislature, begun at Colorado City, July 7, 1862, and adjourned to Denver, July 11, the ordinary school revenue was sought to be supplemented by enacting "That hereafter when any new mineral lode, of either gold bearing quartz, silver, or other valuable metal, shall be discovered in this Territory, one claim of one hundred feet in length on such lode shall be set apart and held in perpetuity for the use and benefit of schools in this Territory, subject to the control of the Legislative Assembly."

This law seemed at the time to promise much for the schools, but the results proved to be insignificant; not one per cent. of the thousands of claims so located ever contributed a dollar to the school fund; a few were sold at prices ranging from five to twenty-five dollars.

By virtue of the provisions of the law of 1861, Mr. W. J. Curtice was, by Governor Gilpin, appointed "Territorial Superintendent of Common Schools" and entered upon the duties of his office December 1st of that year. Mr. Curtice, in the introduction to the school law, published for the use of school officers, says: "The First Legislative Assembly of Colorado, entrusted with the important and varied duties of establishing law and government for our Territory, were not unmindful of its educational interests, and enacted the school law herewith published. That it should be free from imperfections could not reasonably be expected. The school laws of many of our older States, passed after mature deliberation, and amended, as experience dictated from year to year, are still far from perfect. Time and experience, while bringing to light the faults of the present law, will also suggest many improvements, better adapting it to the peculiar requirements of popular education in our new Territory. It now remains for the people and their duly chosen school officers, to immitate the commendable zeal of the Legislative Assembly in behalf of education, by carrying into effect the school law and inaugurating a public school system in every county of the Territory. In discharging this duty, we shall not only remove a great barrier—want of schools—to the rapid settlement of the country, but will be developing an educational system among us, for the future, of greater value than the gold of our mountains, and a better safeguard to society than the electric franchise or standing armies."

It must be borne in mind that the early settlement of Colorado was somewhat anomalous. The pioneers and immigrants of other new regions—Michigan, Illinois, Kansas, etc.—were *families*, seeking permanent homes, while those of Colorado were fortune-hunting men only, whose wives and children were left behind, whose highest ambition and only intentions were to remain here long enough to gather wealth with which to return and enjoy. Schools were not, to them, of much importance, even if there had been the material from which to make them. This condition of things is clearly reflected in Mr. Curtice's instructions to County Superintendents. He says: "In entering upon the discharge of your duties you may find, owing to the absorbing character of the pursuits of many of our people, and the intense application with which every business is followed, that comparatively slight regard will be paid to the interests of education in many localities; and the same might be observed of any other interest unconvertible immediately into money You may not meet with that ready co-operation of the mass of the community in your work that would be desirable; yet, while such a state of things may induce a disposition to withhold time and labor, you will, on the other hand, find no people more ready to contribute the one thing most needful—material aid—in establishing schools in their midst. While our people are more awake to their individual interests than communities elsewhere, no people can be found more alive to the importance of good schools—none who will contribute more liberally to sustain them.

"Bearing these facts in mind, as well as the vast importance of the work in which you are engaged, referring to the law for your guide and authority, be zealous and active in the discharge of your duties and you will be successful."

To the people generally the Superintendent continues: "The lesson first taught by our early statesmen, and successfully enforced by the good and wise who have succeeded them, is substantially this: 'That in proportion as every nation has been enlightened and educated so has been its prosperity. When the heads and hearts of men are generally cultivated and improved, virtue and wisdom must reign, and vice and ignorance cease to prevail; virtue and wisdom are the parents of private and public happiness; vice and ignorance, of private and public misery. This lesson having been taught by the wise and good since the foundation of our Government, and having been carried into practice in the establishment of schools for the education of the children of the mass of the people in a majority of our States, has produced results in the extension of prosperity, intelligence, and happiness exceeding the hopes of the most sanguine, and of anything before seen in the history of the world. While such, however, has been the case in a majority of the States loyal to the Government and constitution of the country, it is equally true that a minority of the States have, to a great extent, been deaf to the teachings of our own greatest statesmen, and while educating the few, have neglected the many; while alive to the pecuniary and political advantages of the few, have been dead to the interests of the common schools and the instruction thereby of the children of the masses. As might have been, and as was anticipated by the great statesmen of the past, the time has come when they have proved themselves disloyal to their Government, and are to-day engaged in an attempt to effect its overthrow. While their energies are directed with the power of desperation against the life of the nation, in the field, the anathemas of their orators and the sarcasm of their politicians are directed against the school systems of the loyal States. But it rejoices the heart of the patriot to believe that the enlightened power of the people, which has made our country what it is, is also equal to the work of maintaining it; and that the day is not far distant when those now in rebellion, learning how vain the attempt to effect its overthrow, will gladly return to the allegiance of a Government that has always been a friend and protector of all its citizens."

The quotation from the words of Colorado's first Superintendent of Schools are reproduced here, not wholly for the true sentiments contained, but as reflecting, in a measure, the condition of affairs, both local and national, at the time the foundation of Colorado's schools was being laid; very little indeed, as might well have been expected, was accomplished in the matter of superstructure during the first administration. The number of school children within the boundaries of the entire territory were not sufficient, had they been gathered into one district, to have formed a first-class district of to-day. Nevertheless there was a beginning, and a good one.

Mr. Curtice resigned his office in 1863, and William S. Walker was appointed to the vacancy. Mr. Walker left no records of his doings, and the presumption is that little or nothing was done in the office, probably from the fact, as above stated, **of an** insufficiency of working material.

At the fourth session of the Legislature, held at Golden City, in 1865, the school law was amended, making the Territorial Treasurer *ex officio* Superintendent of Public Instruction, with an annual salary of $500, and also fixing the **compensation of** County Superintendents at $5 a day for actual services; **prior to** this the Superintendent was paid such a sum as the County **Com**missioners saw fit to allow. By this last enactment the Superintendency fell into the hands of Mr. A. W. Atkins, Territorial Treasurer at that time. There are no reports of his official work. The same may be said of his successors in 1866 and 1867. At **the** fifth session of the Legislature, begun at Golden **City,** January 1, and adjourned to Denver January 2, 1866, **a law was** passed making **it** a misdemeanor to jump mineral claims that had been set apart for schools, or for failing to relinquish such claims as had previously been pre-empted; also, providing for the sale and leasing of school claims, and the investment of the proceeds in United States bonds; also, for giving to the colored people **a** pro rata share of the school fund for the maintenance of separate schools.

In December, 1867, **Mr.** Columbus Nuckolls, by virtue of **his office as** Territorial Treasurer, became Superintendent. His deputy, Mr. E. L. Berthoud, evidently set out with a determina**tion** to bring order out of chaos; still but little was accomplished, as will appear from the statement below made to the Legislature, November 20, 1867. **This being** the first semblance of **a** school report in existence, it is deemed worthy **of a place here in full :**

Univ. of
California

ANNUAL REPORT

OF THE SUPERINTENDENT OF PUBLIC INSTRUCTION OF COLORADO.

OFFICE OF TERRITORIAL SUPT.
OF PUBLIC INSTRUCTION,
GOLDEN CITY, Colo. T., Nov. 20, 1867.

To the Honorable Legislature of Colorado Territory:

GENTLEMEN:—I have the honor to submit the following report of the condition of the public schools of the Territory of Colorado, for the year 1867.

Respectfully, your obedient servant,

COLUMBUS NUCKOLLS,
Ter. Treas. and Supt. Pub. Ins.

STATEMENT.

The reports required by law from the several counties of this Territory have, up to date, been received only from two—Pueblo and Clear Creek Counties—which, consequently, gives me no material upon which I can give the summary of our Territorial schools as required by law. I regret this the more as my deputy and assistant, E. L. Berthoud, began in March, 1867, to require reports of all matters pertaining to our public schools throughout the Territory. To aid and facilitate this, he caused to be printed and personally sent and arranged reports in blank of all the minutiæ, and all matters of interest relating to our public schools, and has distributed them to all the counties, with instructions complete, to enable them to be promptly filled out and returned. Together with the required school reports, he sent blank reports, in accordance with Territorial law, upon which the school mining claims, numbered, named and described, could be reported to the Territorial Treasurer and Superintendent of Public Instruction. In this, however, I have met with no success, receiving reports only from Clear Creek and Gilpin Counties, which, up to date, have alone complied with the law.

I would respectfully suggest to the Hon. Legislature, that, inasmuch as the laws of the Territory, in reference to school mining claims, are either disregarded or disputed, and the disposition of the same and of the proceeds of their sale not properly attended to, and the generous provisions of our Territorial laws, in respect to the special school fund, not adequately guarded or guaranteed to the school fund, that the management, disposition and care of the same in the several mining counties be more rigidly defined and placed beyond the contingency of careless and irresponsible acts, or the indifference of those whose ill-paid services do not incite to more vigilant care of such precious funds as those that accrue to our common schools from the sale of school mining claims. It has been suggested that the bonds of County Superintendents might be submitted for examination and approval to the Territorial Treasurer and Superintendent of Public Instruction, before their acts in relation to the sale and disposition of the school property could be either begun or consummated. I would also state that several counties have never, even when requested, informed the Superintendent of Public Instruction who was or who had been County Superintendent, and that it is not yet known to him whether there are any, in those counties, whose bonds have been filed, or whether there is any responsible county organization.

The laws of our Territory prescribe certain reports and returns to be made yearly, or when asked for by the Territorial Superintendent of Public Instruction, but there is no penalty available to compel such, if neglected. We would respectfully ask that a law be passed, empowering the Superintendent to ask for reports of school funds, mining claims, and all expenditures, at any time, if not punctually made.

Respectfully submitted,

COLUMBUS NUCKOLLS,
Terr. Treas. and Supt. Pub. Ins.

It will be seen from the above that even as late as 1867,

there was far from being a *system* of schools; and also, from the report reproduced below, that two years more of time had produced but little improvement:

SCHOOL SUPERINTENDENT'S REPORT.

Office Territorial Supt. Public Instruction,
Denver, Colo., December 25, 1869.

To the Honorable Legislature of Colorado Territory:

Gentlemen :—I have the honor to submit the following report of the condition of the public schools of the Territory of Colorado:

Upon examining the reports of the County Superintendents which are by law required to be made to the Superintendent of Public Instruction, I find that nearly every one complains that the Secretaries of the District Boards fail to include in their reports all the items which the law requires, and in many cases have entirely neglected to make any report, and I am unable to give any reliable statistics relative to the number of schools, teachers, or pupils.

I have distributed to the County Superintendents copies of the school law and blank reports, and have endeavored to have them become familiar with their duties, in order that our school system might be rendered uniform throughout all the counties of the Territory.

In the execution of the school laws I find several defects, to the correction of which I would respectfully call your attention.

The law requires the County Superintendent to give a certificate to teachers after examination, authorizing them to teach a public school in his county for one year. I would suggest that the law be so amended as to read "not exceeding one year," and thus leave it in the power of County Superintendents to grant certificates for a shorter period than one year.

I think it should also be made the duty of the County Superintendent to make a record of the name, age and date of examination, of all persons examined by them, distinguishing between those to whom they issue certificates and those rejected.

The county shool tax is now apportioned among the different school districts, in proportion to the number of persons therein between the ages of 5 to 21 years, thus giving the same proportions of money to districts in which no schools are held, as to those which maintain schools throughout the entire year. I would suggest that the law be amended so as to make the number of pupils attending schools in the district for the previous year the basis for the apportionment.

Some steps should be taken for the formation of District Libraries, and some plan devised to compel the Secretaries of the District Boards to make their reports to the County Superintendents more promptly, and some penalty prescribed where the County Superintendents fail to report to the Territorial Superintendent within the time required by law.

The increasing population of our Territory renders it imperative that our school system should receive attention, and that the monies collected for school purposes in the different counties should be judiciously applied.

Some appropriation should be made for the purpose of printing the different blanks requisite for the use of the County Superintendents, and the officers of the District Boards.

I would recommend to your honorable body the propriety of making the office of School Superintendent a separate and distinct office, as our population and large increase of children in the Territory seem to demand that the office of School Superintendent be a separate office, and a competent Superintendent of Public Instruction be appointed or elected, and paid a sufficient salary to give our Territorial school system his individed attention. All of which is most respectfully submitted.

Your Obedient Servant,

COLUMBUS NUCKOLLS,
School Superintendent of Colorado.

The chaotic condition of school affairs continued until 1870. It was no uncommon thing for the school funds to be misappropriated by both county and district officers. The burden of the songs of nearly all, who were by law required to make reports was about the same: "Lack of interest," "My predecessor in office has left no records," "I hope to get matters in shape so as to render a complete account next year," "School matters here are in a very bad condition; for the past two years the County Commissioners have neglected to levy a school tax, hence we have no money," etc., etc.

The successors of those thus reporting would write to the same effect.

From the fragmentary documents found in the State Superintendent's office, the following grains of interest have been gathered; to which has been added, so far as the same could be ascertained, the time of the opening of the first school and of the erection of the first school house in each county. No effort has been made to fix these initial points subsequent to the year 1870. The important events that have occurred since the year named are to be found in the published biennial reports of the several Superintendents of Public Instruction, hence it is not necessary to chronicle them here.

Arapahoe County.—Omer O. Kent, Superintendent, reports, in 1869: Receipts from the Treasurer of the county, $11,052.20; expenditures, $7,824.07; balance on hand, $3,228.13. He says: "District No. 1, (East Denver,) has at times been paying rent for four different buildings, and for the most of the time the late Board was acting, three buildings have been used for school purposes and six teachers employed. The enumeration of the county shows the number of persons therein, between the ages of 5 and 21 years, to be 1,139; teachers employed in the county, sixteen in public schools and nearly as many more in seminaries and private schools."

The first public school in this county was opened in the winter of 1862, and was taught by a Mr. Lamb and Miss Indiana Sopris. Mr. O. J. Goldrick kept a small private school in the summer of 1859. The first public school house was built in 1871, on Arapahoe street, between Sixteenth and Seventeenth streets.

Bent County.—In 1869, Miss Mattie Smith taught a private school.

Boulder County.—Robert J. Woodward, Superintendent, 1868, reported thirteen districts, 439 persons of school age, salaries from $30 to $100 a month.

The first public school opened in 1860, Mr. A. R. Brown, teacher. Mr. Brown had taught a private school the winter before. The first school house was built in the fall of 1860. This is claimed to be the first school house built in the Territory—a one-room frame building, which was used also for town and church purposes.

Clear Creek County.—William M. Clark, Superintendent, 1869, reported amount of teachers' fund expended, $2,050; on hand, $755.97; number of schools, 5; teachers employed, 5; persons of school age, 255; attending school, 157. District No. 5 has built a first-class school house at a cost of $2,300.

Conejos County.—The Sisters of Loretto kept a private school in 1870.

Custer County.—The first school was opened in 1870, at Colfax, and taught by William Dyrenforth; in the same year was built the first school house.

El Paso County.—R. Douglass, Superintendent, 1868, reported 6 districts, 235 persons of school age, salaries of teachers from $40 to $60 per month. The first school was opened at Colorado City.

Fremont County.—W. R. Fowler, Superintendent, reported, 1869, 7 districts, 180 persons of school age, salaries from $40 to $75 a month, and "a general indifference in the matter of schools."

Gilpin County.—Thomas Campbell reported, 1868, 5 school districts, 639 persons of school age, 1 school house, worth $200, 9 teachers, salaries from $50 to $150 a month. The first school taught in this county was a private school, by Miss Ellen F. Kendall, in her father's house, in the fall of 1862. A public school was soon after opened, and Miss Kendall gave up her school to assist Mr. Thomas Campbell in its management. In this county was built, 1870, the first *permanent* school houses in Colorado. Central City built a granite house at a cost of $20,000, and Black Hawk, a frame, costing $15,000.

Huerfano County.—Benjamin Doss, Superintendent, wrote, 1869: "Being the first Superintendent in the County, I am at a loss to know how to proceed. * * * I have formed four districts, two of them have schools."

Jefferson County.—M. C. Kirby, Superintendent, reported, 1868, 10 districts, 429 persons of school age, salaries from $33.33 to $87.50.

The first school (private) was taught at Golden City, in the winter of 1860, by Mr. J. Daugherty, 18 pupils attended. The first public school was opened in the same district, in 1863, taught by Miss Bell Dixon. In 1863 a one-story brick school house was built, which was used also by the Governor as an office. It was burned, and another was built on the site.

Larimer County.—James M. Smith, Jr., Superintendent, reported, 1868, 3 school districts, 75 persons of school age, and $160 on hand. The first school (private) was taught in 1864, near the present site of Loveland, by Mrs. A. L. Washburn; her patrons paid her $10 a month. The first public school was opened in the winter of 1865, near Loveland, and taught by Mr. Edward Smith. In 1863 a log school house was built by contributors of labor and material. La Porte also opened a public school in 1865.

Park County.—Louis F. Valiton, Superintendent, reports, 1867, that he has just been appointed to fill the vacancy occasioned by the resignation of H. A. W. Tabor. Oliver P. Allen, Superintendent, 1869, reports 2 districts, 64 persons of school age, salaries from $50 to $75 a month.

Pueblo County.—Rev. Charles H. Kirkbride, Superintendent, reports, 1867, 301 persons of school age, 1 school of 38 pupils, and a small private school. The first school in the county was a private one, kept by a **Mr.** Rickart, in 1862; the first public school was opened in 1863—both in Pueblo.

Saguache County.—A. C. Patton, **Superintendent, 1869, says**: " I am the first who has qualified for the **office of School Superintendent.** * * * There are now 30 children, English and Spanish, between the ages of 5 and 21 years, and $500 in the hands of the County Treasurer."

Summit County.—The first school (private) was taught in Lincoln City, in 1862, by W. R. Pollock. The first public school was opened in Breckenridge, in the summer of 1870, and taught by Mr. Ira Clark. The **first** school house was built at the same time and place.

Weld County.—D. J. Fulton, Superintendent, reported, **1868**, 10 districts, 61 persons of school **age, and $2,000** apportioned to the several districts.

Thus has the story of Colorado's early schools been briefly told up to the year 1870. With this year there seemed to have begun a new era—a transition, **as** it were, from infancy to **youth**; temporary measures and temporary structures gave way to permanency. **The advent of the** railroad this **year** seemed like a new birth; the effects of the success of the smelting works at Black Hawk, which had been in operation two years, were being felt. Confidence and stability began to supplant doubt and makeshifts; it had been completely demonstrated that Colorado was to become more than a mere mining camp, or a series of them. The favorable results of irrigation had demonstrated beyond a doubt that farming was, ultimately, **to play an important part in the settlement of this region.** Irrigating 'canals of great **extent were** projected, colonies were founded, immigration **increased, and all** circumstances tended towards the upbuilding of a great commonwealth. **Costly** public school houses sprang up **as if** by magic. Following those of Central City and Black Hawk, were the still finer structures of Denver, Greeley, Golden, Colorado Springs and Georgetown. Private and sectarian schools and seminaries kept pace with the public schools.

The Legislature of 1870 made provision for a State School of Mines, to be located at Golden City, and also established the office of Superintendent of Public Instruction. The act provided that the Governor, by and with the consent of the Legislative Assembly, should appoint a suitable person to said office, who should hold the same two years and receive a salary of $1,000 a year.

By virtue of this enactment, Governor E. M. McCook appointed Wilbur C. Lothrop Superintendent of Public Instruction. Superintendent Lothrop published his first report December 20, 1871, covering the years 1870-1. Mr. Lothrop was re-appointed to the office by Governor Elbert, in 1872, and continued until July, 1873, when he resigned, and Horace M. Hale was called to the vacancy. In 1874 Governor Elbert re-appointed Mr. Hale, and in 1876 Governor Routt continued him in the office, which he held until November, 1876, when Joseph C. Shattuck, who had been elected by the people under the provisions of the State Constitution, assumed its duties. Mr. Shattuck was again elected in 1878. In 1880 Leonidas S. Cornell was elected to the office. In 1882 Mr. Shattuck again was chosen, and in 1884 Mr. Cornell was elected, who is still (1886) the incumbent.

As a matter of convenient reference, in the future, it is deemed best to give here the line of succession to the Superintendent's office, notwithstanding the fact that it reaches beyond the period intended to be covered by this narration.

These officers have all published biennial reports, giving in detail the condition and progress of the public schools during their respective administrations; hence it is not deemed necessary to continue this history further. In 1885, during the administration of Horace M Hale the State Teachers' Association was organized, whose proceedings, at each of its annual sessions, it is the province of this volume to record.

Part II.

History of the Colorado State Teachers' Association.

1875–1885.

History of the Association.

The history of the Colorado State Teachers' Association begins with December 28, 1875. The detailed proceedings of the first meeting are here printed.

Time has demonstrated the wisdom and intelligence of the members of that Association. Questions of vital moment were asked and discussed. Resolutions embodying the sense of the assembly were the basis of the subsequent action of the State Constitutional Convention and of the First State Legislature, and every recommendation made by the State Teachers' Association at that time was accepted by the State constitutional and legislative bodies.

That the public school system of Colorado is one of the best in the land is generally conceded; the heartiness of support from the people of the State is one great cause of its usefulness, but without the forming and guiding hand of men and women whose education and experience had prepared them intelligently to direct the initial movements, the schools of Colorado could not have reached so high a plane.

The list of members herewith presented contains the names of many who can still be found enrolled as teachers, while others have drifted from that vocation to other lands and other works.

The number of prominent citizens not regularly in the profession that took part in the proceedings of the first meeting, indicates the interest of the public at that time in the common schools of Colorado.

A few names stand out bright above all others, noticeably that of Horace M. Hale, the then Territorial Superintendent, the work of whose hand and heart is evident to-day in every important result in the educational history of the State. Intimate in the beginning with the needs of the community, and with intelligence and judgment unexcelled, he has assisted in framing and supporting all that is good and efficient in the school history of Colorado. He was the first President of the Association.

The proceedings of the first meeting are here detailed.

HIGH SCHOOL BUILDING,
DENVER, COLO, December 28, 1875.

In pursuance of the following call about 150 teachers and friends of education, of Colorado, met in convention at the High School building, Denver, December 28, 1875:

OFFICE SUPT. PUBLIC INTSRUCTION,
DENVER, COLO., November 25, 1875.

On the 28th of December, proximo, the Superintendents, teachers and friends of public schools will meet in convention at the High School, Denver, and remain in session three days. Questions involving the welfare of our school system will be discussed and such measures adopted as may tend to perfect the same. Especially will the necessity of a thorough revision of our school law be considered, etc., etc. A State Teachers' Association will be organized and a portion of the time devoted to institute work.

All are urgently invited to be present and to use their influence to induce others, both male and female, to attend. The meeting will be an important one, and, doubtless, one of profit to those attending. We hope that every county will be largely and ably represented.

H. M. HALE,
Supt. Public Instruction.

The convention was called to order at 2 o'clock p. m. by Hon. H. M. Hale, Territorial Superintendent of Public Instruction.

The doxology, commencing with "Praise God, from whom all blessings flow," was then sung by the audience, Miss Nannie O. Smith presiding at the piano.

Prayer was offered by the Rev. Dr. Lord, of the Presbyterian Church.

The audience then joined in singing the ever popular song of America,

"My country 'tis of thee,
Sweet land of liberty."

Superintendent Hale then addressed the convention, stating the object for which the call had been issued. His highest anticipations were more than realized, in regard to the number and character of those who had personally responded to his call. Certainly no stronger evidence could be adduced that Colorado has earnest and capable workers in the great cause of popular education. It was not intended that this should be a meeting for what more properly belongs to institute work, but if, after the convention work was completed, there was found time for such work, topics would be discussed and class work presented. The principal object was to gather from different minds and experience, plans for future action ; to agree, if possible, upon some course that would tend to unify the school system of the State; that all might labor to accomplish the same end, and thus exert an influence that should be potent. This was the critical time in the history of Colorado for laying a foundation of the public school system, broad and deep, and in such a manner as to endure for all coming time. A pretty fair system was already established, but it was not sufficiently comprehensive; it had answered the purpose very well up to the present time, but now Colorado had outgrown it and demanded more. The present foundation was not such an one as a wise architect would choose upon which to build an enduring superstructure. We wanted liberal provisions incorporated into the State Constitution that should render the school system secure and efficient; we wanted a State Teachers' Association that should meet annually and discuss theories pertaining to educational methods, and problems evolved from practical school work. Our school law should be thoroughly revised, and this assemblage of educators, who certainly ought to know our wants, should take such action as would tend to bring the matter before our legislators. County Superintendents should organize, in their respective counties, Teachers' Institutes, and engage competent instructors to conduct the same, to the end that young teachers might be instructed, by those of large experience, as to the best methods of carrying on the every day class work, and of disciplining the school.

The Superintendent earnestly hoped that as a result of this meeting the initial steps would be taken that would ultimately lead to the accomplishment of all that had been suggested. He then welcomed those who were present from abroad tendering in behalf of the Denver teachers and their friends the hospitalities of their homes, and left the Convention to its own deliberations.

A motion was made and carried to proceed to the temporary organization, with Mr. Hale as Chairman.

Aaron Gove was selected as temporary Secretary, and Miss Sara A. Scott, of Pueblo, and Miss Estelle Freeman, of Denver, as Assistant Secretaries.

A resolution was then passed that the Convention proceed to the organization of a State Teachers' Association.

Mr. Gove moved that a committee of five be appointed by the Chair to draft the necessary documents for such Association, to report at 9 o'clock to-morrow, which was carried.

Mr. C. E. Parks moved that a committee on programme for to-morrow and next day, consisting of five members, be appointed, which was carried, and Mr. Parks was appointed Chairman.

Prof. Haskell thought it very important to raise the question "What can be done to make our school system operative upon the Spanish-speaking people of the Territory?" They constituted one third of our population, and it was very important that something should be done, whether by committee or otherwise.

After further discussion, on motion of Prof. Haskell, a committee of three, to consider the question and report to the Convention in the future, was raised.

A committee of five on reception was then appointed by the Chair as follows: Mr. Donaldson, Miss Smith, Miss Freeman, Miss Peabody and Miss Collier.

Lucinda Washburn

UNIV. OF
CALIFORNIA

An intermission of fifteen minutes was then taken for general handshaking and acquaintanceship.

Mr. Gove moved that the committee on programme be requested to place on their list the lecture by Judge Belford, and poem by W. E. Pabor, of Greeley, for Thursday evening; a sociable for Thursday evening, to close the exercises, and that the Wednesday afternoon exercises be held at the Broadway school.

After considerable discussion, the three branches of the motion were carried, the place of meeting to-morrow evening designated as Mænnerchor Hall.

On motion, Mr. D. Hurd, Chairman of the committee on education in the Constitutional Convention, was invited to address the Convention, and stated that the committee were waiting for this body to give them the cue, and that the action of the Association would be duly weighed and acted upon. He hoped the Association would appoint a committee to confer with the Standing Committee of the Constitutional Convention; such a matter had been proposed before his committee.

A motion was made that a committee be appointed to report as to the best method of improving the present school system.

Mr. Seybold, of Pueblo, offered a substitute. Mr. Gove moved that consideration of the whole subject be postponed, and made the special order for 10 o'clock to-morrow, which was carried.

The Chairman announced the committees as follows:

On Programme—Messrs. Parks and Donaldson, Miss Randall, Mr. Henry and Mr. Carpenter.

On Organization—Messrs. Gove, Orr, Groesbeck, Davis and Baker.

On Spanish-speaking Pupils, etc.—Messrs. Haskell, Sloane and Brown.

The Convention then adjourned.

— 34 —

WEDNESDAY, December 29, 1875.

Convention was called to order at 9 a. m. by the President.

Prayer was offered by Rev. J. M. Sturtevant, which was followed by the Italian hymn, the members joining heartily in the singing.

The report of Committee on Programme, as submitted by Mr. Frank Carpenter, of Georgetown, was then read and adopted.

Mr. Gove, from the Committee on Organization, read the following preamble and constitution of the "Colorado Teachers' Association," which was adopted:

PREAMBLE.

Resolved, That we, the teachers of Colorado, in convention assembled, in order to advance the interests of education and to diffuse a professional and friendly spirit among the teachers of the commonwealth, do now and hereby form a State Teachers' Association.

CONSTITUTION.

ARTICLE I. This Association shall be called the Colorado Teachers' Association.

ART. II. The Association shall hold its meetings annually. Special meetings may be called at any time by the President, at the written request of the Executive Committee.

ART. III. The officers of this Association shall consist of a President, one Vice-President from each judicial district, one Vice President at large, a Secretary, two Assistant Secretaries, a Treasurer and an Executive Committee of three, all of whom shall be elected annually and shall hold their offices until their successors are elected.

ART. IV. It shall be the duty of the President to preside at the regular meetings of the Association, and to attend to the duties incumbent upon said office; and some one of the Vice-Presidents shall preside in case of his absence.

ART. V. The duties of Secretaries and Treasurer shall be such as usually pertain to those offices.

ART. VI. The Executive Committee shall determine the duration of the annual meetings, arrange for the literary exercises, prepare programmes, maks terms with railroads and determine the time and place of meeting, when the same has not been indicated by the Association. They shall hold one meeting during the year, at such time and place as the Chairman may select

ART. VII. This Association shall consist of teachers and of State, county, township and district school officers in Colorado; each member shall sign the constitution and pay one dollar annually Honorary members may be elected at any annual meeting, and may participate in the debates, but not be entitled to vote.

ART. VIII. All officers shall be elected by ballot, except when otherwise ordered by the Association. A majority of the votes shall elect.

ART. IX. This constitution may be altered or amended by a vote of three-fourths of its members present at any regular meeting of the Association.

BY-LAWS.

I. The Standing Committees shall be composed of five members each, and shall be appointed annually by the Chair. They shall be as follows:
1. Committee on Finance.
2. Committee on Resolutions.
3. Committee on School Law.

II. The duties of the Standing Committees shall be those indicated by their titles.

III. During debate this Association shall conform to the laws of deliberative bodies generally.

A motion was made and carried that all persons who had assembled under the call should be considered as members of the Association until it adjourns.

A motion also prevailed that the present officers of the Convention be hereby declared officers of the Association for the current year.

The election of Treasurer being in order, a motion was carried that the choice be made by acclamation. L. G. A. Copley, of Colorado Springs, was then elected unanimously.

A motion was made to make the Association an incorporated body The matter was referred to the Committee on School Laws.

Mr. Gove moved that all be invited to attend the meetings and participate in the debate, and that all so participating be hereby elected honorary members of the Association. Carried unanimously.

Mr. Hale announced that Colonel Ellsworth, President of the Street Railway Company, invited the members to ride on the cars to and from the Broadway School during the afternoon.

The following resolution, submitted yesterday by Mr. Seybold, of Pueblo, came up as the special order:

Resolved, That a standing committee of seven, consisting of the Territorial Superintendent of Public Instruction and six others whom he shall appoint, be instructed to confer with the Educational Committee of the Constitutional Convention, on the educational provisions that should be incorporated in the constitution of the State of Colorado, and with the Educational Committee of the Territorial Legislature.

Mr. Seybold remarked that the nature of the work would be left to the judgment of the committee.

Mr. Morehouse would like the resolution better, if it appointed the Territorial Superintendent Chairman of the committee, with power to select his six associates.

Mr Seybold responded that such was the intent of the resolution.

Mr. **Griffin** would inquire if that would not be placing too much **power** in the **hands of** the Territorial Superintendent?

Mr. **Goff** thought it would be too expensive for seven men to stop in **Denver and confer** with the bodies named. **It was the** general rule for such associations to discuss and adopt resolutions, and thus give legislative **bodies certain** points to act upon.

Mr. **Hale,** Superintendent of Public Instruction, remarked that if the Territorial Superintendent and County Superintendents did **not know the wants** of the different counties **and the whole Territory, he** could not tell who did know them. **Letters had been frequent** recommending **changes** in the school **law.** Some time **ago** a bill had been **drafted** and presented **to the** Legislature, but it was objected **that** the bill gave too much power to the Territorial Superintendent, and it was defeated. He **would** state, however, that he would make up the committee from County Superintendents and district officers.

Mr. Shattuck thought the resolution incomplete. **A committee** would be appointed to work, but no suggestion had been **made** to the Association as to what changes in **the school law** should be made. He thought two committees should be appointed, one to confer with the convention, and the other with the Legislature, to report to-morrow the **skeleton, or** leading features of desired changes.

Mr. **Buell stated** that he had attended the convention **more particularly to engage in** the discussion of the school law. **If something was not** submitted to the Legislature by which **that** body could reform the defects in the present law, the great object of the convention would be defeated. He moved to amend the resolution so the committee would report at ten to-morrow the **skeleton of** the provisions they would recommend to the Legislature, **which** was accepted, and the resolution passed.

Mr. Gove offered the following:

Resolved, **That the** committee that hereafter may be appointed **to confer with the Committee on Education in** the Constitutional Convention be asked to urge **upon their** attention the following points: The school fund shall be sacredly preserved intact, the interest on the same, **only, to be expended**; the sale of such lands as may be **given to the State for educational purposes shall be** postponed, to the end that the proceeds, **in time, may perhaps be** sufficient to maintain public schools without taxation; the constitution shall make it the duty of the Legislature to **provide for the** establishment and maintenance of **a uniform** system of schools, including elementary, normal, preparatory and university departments, such schools to be free to all residents of the State; to provide for the offices of State and County Superintendents; to provide for the establishment of libraries; to provide for the care and education of the blind, mute and feeble minded; **to provide for the establishment of a reform** school; to **cause all instruction to** be imparted through the medium of the English language; to exclude sectarianism, as is set forth as follows in Article VIII, Section 3, of the Illinois Constitution: " Neither the **General Assembly nor any county,** city, town, township, **school** district **or other public corporation,** shall ever make any appropriation, **or pay from** any public fund whatever, anything **in aid of any church** or any sectarian purpose, or to help support or **sustain any school,** academy, seminary, college, university **or other** literary or scientific institution controlled by any church or sectarian denomination whatever; nor shall any grant or donation **of** land, money **or** other personal property ever be made by **the** State for any church or for any sectarian purpose."

Mr. Wilbur took the floor and presented his views at **length** as to what reforms were needed in the school laws.

Professor Haskell moved that Mr. Wilbur's paper be respectfully referred to Hon. **Daniel Hurd, on its own** merits, for the use **or benefit of** the Committee on Education in the Constitutional Convention, which was carried.

Further consideration of **Mr. Gove's resolutions was** postponed until 11 o'clock to-morrow.

Prof. Haskell, from the Committee on Education of Spanish Children, reported resolutions:

WHEREAS, In the opinion of this Convention, it is the province of a proper school **system** in this country to provide the means of a common English education to all our children and youth, of whatever rank, race or sect, and

WHEREAS, It is evident from the Superintendent's report, and from other sources, that our system is practically inoperative among a large portion of the Spanish speaking people of Southern Colorado, therefore

Resolved, That we hereby respectfully ask the Constitutional Convention and both branches of our Legislature to take this subject into kind and special consideration.

Resolved, That our City School Boards would be doing a public favor by inviting the Spanish youth to attend their High Schools free from tuitional charges, with the hope that some of them may become useful teachers in public schools, and that the Spanish language may with propriety be taught, without charge, as the French and English now are.

Resolved, That we commend the study and colloquial use of the Spanish language to our teachers as a means of personal culture, and a source of probable usefulness and pleasure.

Resolved, That a popular compendium of our school system and its modes of usefulness to the rising generation of American citizens of all classes should be prepared and published in Spanish, and circulated among that class of our fellow citizens in whose behalf this report is more especially made.

Consideration was postponed until 10:45 to-morrow.

President Hale here announced the following standing committees:

Finance—Messrs. Donaldson, Harrington, Davis, Buell and Carpenter.

School Laws—Messrs. Shattuck, Millington, Baker, Morehouse and Groesbeck.

Resolutions—Mr. Copley, Miss Washburn, Miss Smith, Mr. Brown and Mr. Orr.

Association adjourned to meet at the Broadway School at 1:30 o'clock.

AFTERNOON SESSION.

A majority of the members of the Association accepted the invitation of Superintendent Ellsworth, of the Street Railway lines, and were conveyed to the new Broadway School, where the afternoon session was held.

It was 2 o'clock before the services were opened with a chant, "The Lord's Prayer."

This was followed by an essay by Mr. W. A. Henry, of Boulder, on "My Hobby—A Plea for a Happier Method of Teaching in our Common Scools."

Mr. Hale was of opinion that the leading and most admirable sentiment of the essay was to teach pupils the beauties of good books, so that they would be hungry for more of them.

Mr. Henry added that, in country towns where there were no public libraries, all good books which the owners were willing to lend should be collected and distributed among the pupils. They were doing that in Boulder with great success.

Mr. Boyd remarked that the great danger was that, in cultivating the taste for literature, it was so apt to chain the attention that the study in the school room would be endangered.

Superintendent Hale, in alluding to portions of the essay, instanced a school house which had recently been erected, wherein the school rooms were but twenty feet square, and yet were seated for forty pupils. The unhealthfulness of such rooms, so contracted simply to save money, might be inquired into by some school directors whom he saw present. The accommodation afforded to each pupil in that structure was but one-half that furnished in the Broadway building, and yet every one could see the latter was not too roomy for the comfort and health of the pupils.

A motion was made and carried that the essay reflected the sentiments of the Association, and that the same be handed to the Secretary for publication.

The same disposition, on motion, was made of Mr. Henry's essay on reading.

Mr. Copley moved that the Association proceed to the consideration of the resolutions offered by Mr. Gove in the morning, which was carried.

Mr. Boyd moved that the topics be taken up by sections.

The first section, that the school fund be sacredly preserved intact, and the interest only expended, was adopted without debate.

The section that the Constitutional Convention be asked to postpone the sale of the lands given to the State for educational purposes until such time as the interest of the fund shall support the schools without taxation, was taken up. Several members were of opinion that the money would increase faster by selling the lands and placing the fund on interest.

Mr. Hurd thought that some provision should be made so that proper safeguards would be thrown around the sale of the lands. He thought that the lands, if sold now, would return very little revenue; but in time would furnish a fund sufficient to educate all the children of the State.

Professor Haskell stated that the question was a complicated one, and if the section was passed it might do a great deal of damage. He referred to cases where a portion of school sections, or school property, could be sold, and by the improvements thus secured the residuum would be increased in value to an amount greater than the original value of the whole property.

Mr. Gove replied that there was nothing in the resolution to prevent the leasing of such property.

The discussion continued in the same vein for half an hour, when a motion to lay the section on the table was made and lost.

The section was then adopted.

The section requesting the Constitutional Convention to require a uniform system of free schools, was adopted.

The section providing for the offices of State and County Superintendents was passed.

Also, the one providing for public libraries.

Also, providing for the education of the blind, mute and feeble minded.

Also, the article providing for a Reform School.

Also, to cause all instruction to be imparted through the medium of the English language.

The provision excluding sectarianism, and adopting the provision of the Illinois constitution, was postponed until to-morrow.

An invitation to the night exercises at Mænnerchor Hall was cordially extended to all in attendance.

The Association then adjourned until 9 o'clock to-morrow at the High School building.

EVENING SESSION.

The attendance at Mænnerchor Hall was both an ovation to the Teachers' Association and to the school authorities who had planned the exercises. About 7 o'clock the stream of people commenced pouring into the hall, until every available seat was occupied with the first citizens of Denver and the visitors to the Convention. The difficulty in providing for the vast throng prevented the opening of proceedings earlier than 7:45 o'clock, when Mr. Hale, President of the Teachers' Association, ascended the platform and after apologizing for the necessity of dispensing with the music promised in the programme, remarked that he desired to allude to the object of the present Convention, and to say a word in behalf of the public schools. He stated that there were 20,000 school children in the Territory, and yet during the past year only one-half that number had entered a school room, and only one-half of that half had attended school 116 days in the year. This fact of itself showed that there was something egregiously wrong, and that the interest in education should be increased. Hence the Convention had been called to draw the attention of the people to the facts as they existed. No motives of selfishness or personal benefit had brought these teachers together. "Why," said he, "I know a school district in the Territory where 300 school children are resident, and yet but fifty of them have attended school during the past year."

The people should give the matter their earnest attention, and see if more encouragement and practical aid could not be given in those districts where school houses are building, and where efforts are making to increase the interest in the education of the children. That had been the object of the Convention, and was the aim of the present entertainment. He then introduced to the vast audience Mr. W. E. Pabor, of Greeley, who would recite a poem, and Judge Belford, of Central, who would deliver an address.

THURSDAY'S SESSION.

Previous to the opening of the regular session, President Hale remarked that before calling the meeting to order he had a few suggestions to make. He desired authority to appoint the Committee of Conference on the School Law rather early, and he wished to meet the County Superintendents after the session of the afternoon. There was so much business to be transacted during the day that he hoped each member would put in the time to the best advantage, without unnecessary talking. He was very anxious to finish the work as it had been begun, and suggested the programme as made out for the day be waived that this might be accomplished.

The session was opened with prayer by Rev. Mr. Stewart, of Golden, and the singing of the "Portugese Hymn."

On motion, the programme made out for the day was waived.

Mr. Gove remarked that he knew from experience that it was pleasant for Teachers' Associations to receive congratulatory words from sister bodies. The Illinois State Teachers' Association was now in session at Rock Island. He therefore moved that the Colorado body should authorize the President to send a congratulatory telegram to the Illinois Association, which was carried unanimously.

Mr. Hale sent the following message

W. B. Powell, President Illinois State Teachers' Association, *in Session at Rock Island, Illinois :*

The mountains to the valley, greeting. Our initial meeting. One hundred teachers present.

H. M. HALE,
President Colorado Teachers' Association.

President Hale received the following response to his telegram:

ROCK ISLAND, ILLS., Dec. 30, 4 p. m.

H. M. Hale, President Colorado Teachers' *Association :*

The teachers of Illinois return greeting to their brethren on the mountains. Your's is a grand birth, on the eve of a new '76.

W. B. POWELL,
President Illinois State Teachers' Association.

Mr. Wilbur moved that the Association take up the discussion of the ninth section of Mr. Gove's resolution, prohibiting sectarianism in public schools, which was carried.

Mr. Wilbur moved that the President be invited to participate in the discussion, which was carried.

Mr. Boyd moved the adoption of the last section of the resolution, prohibiting sectarianism.

Mr. Copley moved to amend the section by authorizing the Legislature "to prohibit the exclusion of the Bible."

Mr. Boyd offered as a substitute the following·

"That the Legislature pass such laws as will completely secularize education."

Mr. Gove was sorry that the question of the introduction of the Bible into the public schools had been raised, and he was confident that after three hours' discussion the views of no member will be changed, and also that no measure passed by this Association would influence any member of either the Convention or the Legislature. He knew the sentiment of the people on the subject was very much divided, but that sentiment was decided, and the matter should be left to the Convention.

Mr. Boyd was just as willing as any one to leave the matter to the Constitutional Convention. He had offered the substitute merely to place the matter on a clear basis. The word "sectarianism" was ambiguous, but the word "secularize" was not.

Mr. Copley said the amendment had been offered in order that the sentiment of the teachers might be gained. He wanted to know whether the motto of the school room should be "Nothing Without God," or "Nothing With God." He was willing to take the vote on the matter just now.

Mr. Goff said the word "secularize" had one merit. All could know what it meant. It takes all religion out of merely education, and that goes further than taking the Bible out of the schools. It expunges religion from all history and all branches of education.

Miss Merritt remarked that to exclude the Bible from the avenues of education would be to exclude general history, as the Bible was the foundation upon which all laws rested. There should be some decided standard upon which the morals of the child could stand.

Rev. Mr. Bliss was about speaking, when Mr. Shattuck raised the point that the special order for 10 o'clock, which hour had arrived, was the appointment of the committee to confer with the Constitutional Convention and the Legislature. His point was sustained, and the President announced the following as the committee:

H. M. Hale, Chairman; J. C. Shattuck, Aaron Gove, P. E. Morehouse, J. B. Groesbeck, W. A. Donaldson and T. A. Sloane.

Rev. Mr. Bliss then said that he believed as much as any one in the doctrine of separating church and State in its true interpretation; still, he also believed that the Bible was the foundation of all morals, and the foundation upon which the American republic was erected. Good citizens could not be made by making them pagans. Pagan republics must always die. The question affected the very life of the Nation. He was opposed to sectarianism in the schools and against dividing the school money, but the matter of the use of the Bible in the schools affected him as a citizen and a tax payer, in so far as it inculcated good morals.

Mr. Shattuck, in referring to the formal reading of the Bible in the schools, and the fact that such routine work had little to do with the inculcation of good morals and true reverence for religion, gave a short history of the St. Louis public schools, where the subject had been ignored, and the success and thoroughness of which schools were not excelled in the country.

Mr. Haskell offered the following substitute:

Resolved, That no law shall be passed requiring the daily reading of the Bible in the public schools, nor to exclude it therefrom.

Mr. Hale thought the discussion had proceeded far enough, as there were other more practical questions, such as the proposed amendments to the school law, and although he was full of the sublimity of the topic, he thought the business interests of the Association demanded the vote should be taken at once, as the views of no member were likely to be changed by the discussion. He, therefore, moved the previous question, which was carried.

Mr. Haskell's substitute was then passed.

Some discussion having arisen as to whether the passage of Mr. Haskell's substitute set aside the original section offered by Mr. Gove, re-affirming the constitutional provision of Illinois, Mr. Haskell remarked that he did not understand that it did; that it left the proposition of the resolution intact, and was passed only as an expression of the opinion of the Association, to go to the committee in company with Mr. Gove's resolution.

The President decided that both Mr. Haskell's substitute and Mr. Gove's resolution had passed.

Mr. Shattuck offered a resolution that the Executive Committee be authorized to publish, in pamphlet form, the address of Judge Belford, at Mænnerchor Hall, together with the poem read by Mr. W. E. Pabor.

Mr. Haskell moved to amend by printing, also, the action of the Association on sectarianism.

A substitute was offered that the proceedings of the Convention be printed, together with the poem and address, which was carried.

Mr. Wilbur offered the following, which was passed after some discussion:

Resolved, That we desire the Constitutional Convention to provide for a fixed State tax for school purposes, to the end that schools may be permanent in character.

Another proposition, presented by Mr. Wilbur, was passed, and read as follows:

"Also, that all special or local legislation in relation to schools be forever prohibited."

A third proposition, offered by Mr. Wilbur, on motion of Mr. Stewart, was laid on the table. It read as follows:

"Also, that that part of the fund that, in proportion to numbers, belongs to the lower grades in graded schools, be exclusively applied to them."

Mr. Seybold offered the following, which, on motion of Mr. Stewart, was referred to the committee to confer with the convention and Legislature:

Resolved, That we, as a Convention of educators, do earnestly urge upon our Legislature to enact such laws as will secure to each and every child in our Territory the advantage of at least a common school education in the English language.

Mr. Haskell, Chairman of the Committee on the Education of Spanish Pupils, called up the resolutions reported by the committee, which were printed in the *Tribune*, and moved the adoption of the same.

Mr. Bliss moved to amend by referring the resolutions to the Committee on Conference, which was lost.

The resolutions were then adopted.

Mr. Haskell moved to add to the first resolution the following, which was carried:

"And we suggest the propriety of employing a Spanish

speaking Assistant Superintendent, to labor three months in each of the next three years, to encourage our Mexico-Spanish citizens in developing the English school system among them, for the benefit of their children."

Mr. Shattuck moved that the Association proceed to take up the recommendations to the Legislature. The time set for the session was rapidly passing away, and the important work of legislative suggestions had not been touched. The motion was carried.

Mr. Boyd offered the following, which was passed:

Resolved, That this Association recommend House Bill No. 106, presented by the lower branch of the last Legislature, as the basis of a school law to be passed by the present Legislature.

The bill as recommended was then taken up section by section. When the fifth section came up, requiring the Superintendent to visit the schools once in every two years, an amendment was adopted providing that the visits be either by the Superintendent "or his deputy."

The seventh section of the bill, which empowers the Territorial Superintendent to remove County Superintendents for cause, and which was stricken out in the Lower House because it gave the Territorial Superintendent too much power, came up.

Mr. Bliss thought the objections could be answered by modifying the section so that the Territorial Superintendent might bring charges before the County Commissioners, and give them the power to remove.

Mr. Shattuck was confident the section would not pass, and probably should not. The people were very jealous of any interference with officers elected by them at the ballot box. It was probably natural that they should be. He would prefer that if the people of a county elect a *non compos* officer, they should suffer the penalty of that election through his inefficient acts.

Judge Leland here addressed the Convention and stated that he held in his hand a petition to the Constitutional Convention from Clear Creek, providing for the impeachment of various officers for causes stated, which would include County Superin-

UNIV. OF
CALIFORNIA

tendents, and which would probably do away with the necessity for passing the section.

Mr. Wilbur **moved that the** seventh section of the bill be **laid** on the table, which was carried.

The remaining portions of the bill, relating to County Superintendents and school officers generally, were then passed, when, the hour for adjournment having arrived, the Convention took a recess until half past 1 o'clock.

The afternoon session opened with a full attendance at 2:45.

Dr. Groesbeck **moved that the** Executive Committee be requested to call the next annual meeting of the Association at **the** University Building, in Boulder, which was carried.

Mr. Donaldson offered the following resolution, which **was passed**:

Resolved, That the money in the hands of the Treasurer **of** this Association be handed over to the Executive Committee, **to** be used in defraying the expenses of the Association.

Mr. Baker moved that a **committee of five be appointed to** nominate officers for the next year, which was carried.

President Hale appointed the following as the committee: Messrs. Baker, of Denver; Carpenter, of Clear Creek; **Annis, of** Greeley; Stewart, of Golden, and Copley, **of** Colorado Springs.

THE SCHOOL LAW

Title second, of the School Bill, concerning **the Territorial** Board of Education, came up in order.

Mr. Wilbur offered an amendment to the ninth section, in reference to the organization of the Board. It provides that the Territorial Board shall consist of **the** Superintendent of Instruction, and two members from each judicial district, to be elected by the Legislature. The amendment was passed, and the section adopted as amended.

Section eleven of the bill providing for a uniform series of text books, which after being adopted shall **not be** changed for a period of four years, came up for passage.

Mr. Gove strongly opposed **the section as a** very dangerous one, inviting bribery from publishers, and engrafting a system which had proved a failure in California, Nevada and many other localities.

Mr. Hale confessed that in embodying the section **he had been** largely influenced by outside pressure, yet he could not see how the public could be damaged by its passage. The merit of any book was the only recommendation that it possessed.

The section was stricken out.

The section referring to the qualification and examination of applicants for Teacher's Certificates coming up. Mr. Orr moved that the examination be enlarged so as to embrace Vocal Music.

Miss Merritt moved to amend the amendment by including **also,** examination on the Constitution of the United States, which **last amendment** was agreed to.

Mr. Orr's amendment **was not agreed to.**

The section, as amended, was then passed.

The section touching the granting of Graded Certificates, on **motion of Dr. Groesbeck,** was amended so that no **Teacher's Certificate should be renewed** without examination, except those which were of the first grade.

The section touching the duties of County Superintendents was amended in so far that the County Superintendent be required to submit **the** record of his official proceedings to the County Commissioners at least once a year.

The section in reference to the administration of the official oath **to** School Directors and Teachers, and vesting such administration in **the** County Superintendent, was amended **so that a** member of **the** outgoing Board **could administer the oath to the incoming Board.**

An amendment allowing a **Union High School** to be formed in any County, upon certain formula, without regard to the number of scholars attending the common schools, was passed.

Mr. Gove offered a resolution in regard to the duty of the School Board, as follows, which was passed:

Resolved, That it shall be one of the duties of District Boards to direct what text **books and** apparatus shall be used in the several schools, and strictly to enforce uniformity of text books therein, but shall not permit text books to be changed oftener than once in four years.

The remaining sections of the bill were then referred to the committee appointed to confer with Committees of the Constitutional Convention and Territorial Legislature.

On motion, the Secretary was directed to forward to each member of the Association a copy of the proceedings of this Convention, together with the report of the Committee of Conference, if practicable.

Mr. Baker, from the committee to suggest officers for the next year, submitted the following list:

President, Aaron Gove, Denver.

Vice-Presidents, A. J. Wilbur, Greeley; F. A. Sloane, Pueblo; at large, J. C. Shattuck, Greeley; P. E. Morehouse, Georgetown.

Secretary, Miss E. J. Merritt, Colorado Springs.

Assistant Secretaries, Miss E. H. Shumway, Georgetown; Mr. W. A. Henry, Boulder.

Treasurer, L. G. A. Copley, Colorado Springs.

Executive Committee, H. M. Hale, Denver; A. B. Orr, Golden; J. H. Baker, Denver.

On motion the report was adopted, and the officers elected.

RESOLUTIONS.

Mr. L. G. A. Copley, Chairman of the Committe on Resolutions, submitted the following, which were passd unanimously:

Resolved, That the thanks of this Association are due to Superintendent H. M. Hale for the able manner in which he has conducted its deliberations.

Resolved, That the thanks of this Association are due to the people of Denver who have entertained us so kindly during our attendance at this Convention.

Resolved, That the thanks of this Convention are hereby tendered to the various railroad and stage lines centering in this city, for their reduction of fare to members of this body.

Resolved, That we thank Col. Ellsworth for his liberality in giving us the free use of the street cars to and from the sessions of this Convention at the Broadway School House.

Resolved, That our especial thanks are hereby tendered to Aaron Gove, the City Superintendent, and the Board of Education of East Denver for the use of the High and Broadway School Buildings.

Resolved, That our thanks are due the press for the interest shown in the work, and for the very ready manner in which they have advertised and reported the proceedings of the Association from its beginning to its close.

Resolved, That the thanks of this body are tendered to Judge Belford for his lecture, and W. E. Pabor for his poem, delivered before this Association.

L. G. A. COPLEY,
ALBERT B. ORR,
F. M. BROWN,
L. WASHBURNE.

The Convention then adjourned *sine die.*

The following were elected Honorary Members:

Gov. John L. Routt,	Hon. J. C. Wilson,
J. B. Belford,	R. W. Woodbury,
Dr. B. F. Crary,	Dr. Willis Lord,
Amos Bixby,	N. C. Meeker,
Dr. R. G. Buckingham,	Stephen Decatur,

Hon. Wilbur F. Stone.

The members with their friends and citizens gathered in the High School on Thursday evening for a social. Although no set programme had been arranged, yet three hours were spent in a general good time, enhanced by the supply of refreshments furnished by a few friends.

At eleven o'clock the party retired, the last act being the singing of "Auld Lang Syne."

The following are the names of those who joined the Colorado Teachers' Association at its First Annual Meeting:

Annis, Frank J.,	Greeley.
Askew, W. T.,	Denver.
Adriance, Miss Nellie	Denver.
Ashley, E. M.,	Denver.
Allen, N. E.,	
Baker, James H.,	Denver.
Bryant, Louise V.,	Colorado Springs.
Beecher, Ella P.,	Colorado Springs.
Buel, G. W.,	Golden.
Brundige, Miss M. L.,	Denver.
Boyd, David,	Greeley.
Bliss, T. E.,	Denver.
Brown, A. G.,	Central.
Brown, Francis M.,	Black Hawk.
Brainerd, Julia D.,	Colorado Springs.
Bradley, Julia M.,	Central.
Carpenter, Frank R.,	Georgetown.
Carpenter, Mrs. Frank R.,	Georgetown.
Copley, L. G. A.,	Colorado Springs.
Chambers, J. T.,	Denver.
Collier, Mrs. G. M.,	Denver.
Dill, Mrs. Helen,	Denver.
Devinny, Miss Lizzie,	Denver.
Donaldson, W. A.,	Denver.
Defrance, Mattie A.,	Denver.
Davis, F. B.,	Longmont.
Day, E. A.,	Longmont.
Freeman, Miss Estelle,	Denver.
Fullerton, Alice,	Nevada.
Fullerton, W. C.,	Nevada.
Gove, Aaron,	Denver.
Groesbeck, J. B.,	Golden.
Garbutt, E. N.,	La Porte.
Ganiard, Sarah M.,	Denver.

Griffin, James V., ... Morrison.
Gottesleben, Peter, ... Denver.
Garbutt, Mrs. M. E., ... Denver.
Glave, Paul C., ... Denver.
Haskell, T. N., ... Denver
Harrington, Isaac B., ... Littleton.
Harmon, H. R., ... Boulder
Hahn, S. B., ... Central.
Hurd, Daniel, ... Denver.
Hale, H. M., ... Denver.
Henry, W. A., ... Boulder.
Howard, Oliver, ... Greeley.
House, Mrs. E. P., ... Evans.
Hannah, Kate L., ... Denver.
Hannum, Miss M. E., ... Denver.
Hersey, J. Clarence, ... Valmont.
Kenney, Mrs. Margaret, . . . Denver.
Keith, T. M., ... Valmont.
Laty, Wm. D., ... Greeley.
Lothrop, W. C., ... Denver.
Murray, D. B., ... Golden.
Moorehouse, E. P., ... Georgetown.
Moorehouse, Mrs. E. P., . . . Georgetown.
Merritt, Ellen J., ... Colorado Springs.
McGill, Mary, ... Central City
Morrison, Anna A., ... Golden.
Millington, F. C., ... Denver.
Moulton, Fred. A., ...
McCreery, W. H., ... Loveland.
McMurty, M. E., ... Denver.
Merrill, Miss Viola, ... Denver.
Newton, W. M., ... Denver.
Orr, Albert B., ... Golden.
Parks, Chas. E., ... Denver.
Pabor, Wm. E., ... Greeley.
Parkinson, C. E, ... Castle Rock.

Presley, James N., ... Silver Plume.
Phillips, Ivers, ...
Roy, Mrs. S. K., ... Denver.
Robinson, Ellen J., ... Black Hawk.
Randall, Miss Frona, ... Denver.
Strong, Wm. J., ... Castle Rock.
Shattuck, Joseph C., ... Greeley.
Sloane, Theodorea A., ... Pueblo.
Storms, H., ... Denver.
Seybold, Gilbert A., ... Pueblo.
Scott, Sarah A., ... Pueblo.
Smith, Nannie O., ... Denver.
Seacord, Lydia M., ... Georgetown.
Shumway, Elizabeth H., . . . Georgetown.
Stewart, R. L., ... Golden.
Shields, Hattie E., ... Colorado Springs.
Stuart, R. S., ...
Selby, Miss Martha, ... Denver.
Thomas, Mary, ... Central City.
Tibbals, Miss Sarah E., . . . Denver.
Williams, E. Cone, ... Boulder.
Woolman, N. E., ... Denver.
Washburne, Lucinda, ... Georgetown.
Watters, L. H., ... Denver.
Wells, C. L., ... Denver.
Wilber, Alvin J., ... Greeley.
Wilson, J. M., ... Denver.
Wadleigh, Elizabeth E., . . . Colorado Springs.
Westover, Miss C. M., ... Denver.
Youngman, G. F., ... Boulder.

A list of the Presidents of the first ten meetings is given below, together with the place at which each meeting was held:

H. M. Hale, Denver, ... First Meeting.
Aaron Gove, Boulder, ... Second Meeting.
Joseph C. Shattuck, Denver, . Third Meeting.

Lucinda Washburn, Denver, . Fourth Meeting.
J. A. Sewall, Denver, ... Fifth Meeting.
James H. Baker, Denver, . . Sixth Meeting.
Isaac C. Dennett, Colo. Springs, Seventh Meeting.
J. S. McClung, Pueblo, . . . Eighth Meeting.
H. M. Hale, Greeley, ... Ninth Meeting.
David Boyd, Denver, ... Tenth Meeting.

The policy of the Association with regard to places at which the annual meeting should be held is indicated by the above list. While Denver is the most convenient, both with regard to transportation and rooms for meetings, a desire has at several times been manifested to meet in other cities.

The reflex influence of such a gathering of teachers upon the community is a power to be considered.

Six of the ten meetings have been at Denver, the other four were at Boulder, Colorado Springs, Pueblo and Greeley.

SECOND MEETING.

The second meeting at Boulder will never be forgotten by the pilgrims who did penance on their journey thitherward. The discomfort of spending one day and night on the railroad, the train being stopped by snow, and nothing to eat until a locomotive brought, towards morning, boxes of crackers from the rear, contributed to an experience not remembered with pleasure. The songs and jests and choruses of that tired, hungry crowd of teachers on the Colorado Central Railroad, on the night of the second of January, 1877, made a page in the history of the Association.

Arriving at Boulder, and landing on the houseless plain a mile away from town, with no person to receive or point out the way, satchels in hand, they walked that cold, weary mile before sunrise on a winter morning, and arrived at the hotel to find little room. The people of the town did not choose generally to entertain such guests, even when financial remuneration was offered.

Late in the forenoon of the day of arrival a few score gathered in the church, and the second session was commenced. The Association has not met in Boulder since that time.

From the President's address at that time the following extracts are taken:

"For people of noble and patriotic purposes the world ever turns, unconciously, first to mountaineers. The Old World has given abundant evidence that whatever may be said of people of the lowlands, the denizens of high and rugged countries are ever eminent for integrity and enterprise. Thirty years from to-day the pupils of Colorado public schools will be the product of a people made up of the very best elements of the world, bred and trained in the purest air, and under the brightest sky of earth, surrounded by the comforts of a plenteous civilization, without its attendant evils."

SCHOOL HOUSES.

"Again, upon the basis of finance depends the building of school houses, and how many will be erected in Colorado in the immediate future! What kind of a house? How expensive? What its interior arrangement? What its external appearance? If in your district an enterprise of this sort is discussing and you are not consulted, you may accept the fact as evidence of weakness. An architect will plan the house, the Board will accept the plans, and the teacher who occupies his proper position will be permitted materially to advise. What shall we advise? A building with two floors, never more, staircases open and every stair in sight from either floor, ample heating and ventilating apparatus, comfortable seatings, ample wardrobe and proper light. The people sometimes call for towers and elaborate belfries; the architect will insist upon a proper architectural effect and display, while we will say, give us a comfortable, reasonable house with good teachers; never mind the sky-scrapers, long flights of stairs and magnificent exteriors. Beautiful buildings will never make effective schools. Our advice will not all be followed, but you and I, fellow teachers, have it in our power to save for our young State hundreds of thousands of dollars within the next ten years, by taking a position against elaborate and expensive school buildings made for ornament and show rather than for use."

PAY AS YOU GO.

"Shall we do what we can towards having as fine buildings as we can afford, but never sacrifice style, emulation or ambition in building, to debt? One dollar due in twenty years at 10 per cent. interest sold to-day for eighty cents. How far does a dollar go that way? Let us vote bonds when we can't help ourselves. Let us keep our school finances healthy, and success in common school work is assured; with a great debt comes, sure as sunrise, weak teachers, poor schools, apathy among the people, and death."

DISHONEST WORK.

"The reputation of a school is not to be relied upon unless years have been occupied in making it. When our young schools in Colorado are pronounced excellent it behooves us to look well to the work.

"The sentiment of a district made and pronounced in a few weeks or months, expressive of the excellence of the public school, is built upon unstable notions. In physics, no one dare judge of the merits of a machine until the product thereof has been produced and tested. So, with schools, no one can say they are excellent until their product has been sent out to form a constituent part of the community. True, there are many signs of a good school, as there are tokens of a good fruit tree, but the final, complete decision must be reserved for the appearance of the fruit."

THE SCHOOLS ARE THE PEOPLE'S.

"We must not forget that the schools are the people's, not ours, and that the ultimate directive force lies in the people, so that do we wish for reform or change, the expressed opinion of the people should precede action in school affairs. This doctrine is not altogether palatable, when one thinks of the hundred conflicting opinions, and of the approximate truth that every district contains a few individuals who are sure they can conduct your school infinitely better than you do, but we are to take the world as we have found it; we cannot remake it."

The entire proceedings and papers of the first and second meetings were printed by the State Superintendent, without expense to the Association. Since that time no complete record has been printed. The papers read in those years are as admirable and as instructive to the profession to-day as they were at the time written. "Written Work," by I. C. Dennet; "The Kindergarten; Its Aims and Methods," by Emma C. Barrett; "Higher Education in Colorado," by David Boyd; "Essential Incentives to Labor," by Lucinda Washburne, and "The Influence of the Newspaper Press on Education," were essays that have all been preserved in the pamphlet of proceedings of that year.

The important resolutions passed by the Association from time to time, and which really make the platform of the Association, are herewith presented.

The same spirit of earnest endeavor to do the best thing in the best way, characterizes the whole life of the institution.

"*Resolved*, That we, as members of this Association, are heartily in sympathy with the State University in its work of education, and will do what we can to inspire an interest in its behalf among the people." 1877.

"*Resolved*, That we commend the State University and its interests to the careful and persistent nurture of the State authorities." 1879.

"*Resolved*, That we regard that legislation as unfortunate, whereby the provision for higher education at the expense of the State is now dissipated by division of funds amongst three distinct institutions; That we believe the highest interests of public education would be subserved by a consolidation of the three State institutions: School of Mines, School of Agriculture, and State University, under the management of one Board of Control and Direction, thereby giving to each one the advantage of all, and avoid the expense of maintaining often three chairs of scien-

— 60 —

tific investigation, when one would accomplish the same amount and kind of instruction; that we urge upon the Legislature the importance of well equiping and munificently maintaining these schools as the surest and safest guaranty of the prosperity of our commonwealth; that we repeat our resolution of two years ago, viz.: That a State Reform School for boys is needed in Colorado, and that that system known as the family system is preferable to the old custom of congregating the inmates in one large community or building; That the hearty good wishes of this Association go with the retiring State Superintendent of Public Instruction, and that we recognize that during his four years' faithful service the cause of public education in Colorado has reached a higher plane and maintained a prominent position in the country largely through his intelligent supervision." 1880.

THIRD MEETING.

The third meeting was held at Denver, January 3 and 4, 1876. Hon. Jos. C. Shattuck delivered the President's address. The following names and subjects appear upon the programme of that meeting:

Ella P. Beecher—"Conducting Recitations."
Joseph Brinker, sen.—"Moral and Social Education."
Oliver Howard—"That Boy, John!"
Nelly Lloyd Knox—"Lesson in Geography."
Helen McG. Ayres—"Spelling."
W. F. Wegener—"Natural Science."
Jennie Fish—"Ventilation."
Ira W. Davis—"School Attendance."
R. S. Roeschlaub—"School Architecture."
W. J. Waggener—"Text Books."
A. E. Chase—"The Teacher as a Citizen."
G. W. Buell—"Same Old Rut."

The Executive Committee were: Messrs. Aaron Gove, H. L. Parker, and P. E. Morehouse.

The address of the **President** was an excellent **document**, discussing among other important issues the **tendency of Legislatures to enact** compulsory education laws.

After quoting from eminent school authorities on the subject, he **closes** the discussion in these words:

"**In** our neighboring **State of** Kansas such a law has also been **tried and** found wanting.

"**In** the Superintendent's **report for 1876 I find a report on this point from forty-nine counties, forty-one of which declare the law a complete failure; in only three is it** called a success, and **in five a** partial **success, in that it increases the** attendance **by the moral** influence **which it exerts. What is** remarkable **in this respect is** that **only one County Superintendent** expresses **himself as opposed to the law in theory, while many proclaim their devotion to the idea while** reporting the **law a "dead** letter." **There are few persons that** possess sufficient educational enthusiasm, **or that take enough interest in their neighbors'** affairs to be willing **to incur their displeasure by complaining of** them. The fame of **the man who made a fortune by minding his** own **business has reached the rural districts. Is it not then** settled as definitely **as anything can be, by extensive and costly** experiments, **that no compulsory educational law can be made** operative among **American citizens? Is it necessary to add a** Colorado **law to the wrecks that lie** stranded **along this shore? I** have friends **here** this morning who are, **or have been, earnest** advocates **of such a** law. **If any of them are not satisfied with the exhibit I have given, let them come to my** office and **I will feed them on** such **reports till** they cry, '**Hold,** enough!'

" **Let us first** have **school-houses** enough for all, and in them schools, **attractive,** efficient **and** free; if then there be found a **portion of our population untouched by our** educational system, **then, certainly not till then, may we** 'go out into the highways **and hedges** and compel **them to come in,' by** law.

"**Let us** have no more attempts to find the last term of **our series till we** have the first term and the ratio."

FOURTH MEETING.

The fourth meeting was held at Denver, January 2 and 3, 1879. The President, Miss L. Washburn, presided, and delivered the annual address. This was filled with a general review of education from the beginning of the world to the present time. The report touched upon the manner in which schools were conducted in ages past, and compared with the present generation; how the Greeks and Romans made education subservient to their religion, etc.

Miss Washburn referred to a clause in the German school law, which says that "private schools may be opened in Prussia, but must come under State Supervisors, and teachers of such schools must be examined and receive permits to teach by the Government authorities. Also, pupils of such schools must be subject to examination by the State Regents." The speaker suggested that such means should be taken to educate the children of America. She also cited a law now on the statute books of Connecticut which reads "that the town shall pay for the schooling of the poor, and all deficiencies."

Compulsory education in some states has not proved a success, as the labors of some school officers have almost exclusively been confined to looking after truant absentees from the schools.

Her address concluded with a concise review of education for generations, and was fully appreciated by the teachers present.

Rev. W. R. Alger delivered an address to the Association in the evening.

The papers and authors at this meeting are as follows:

W. R. Thomas—"Political Science in the Common School."
Miss M. A. Pease—"Grammar."
N. E. Garbutt—"Education."
Miss S. C. White—"Phonetic Work in Primary Schools."

Mr. Hershberger—"Odds and Ends."
Miss E. Sabin—"Language."
I. C. Dennett—"Discipline."
F. J. Annis—"Struggle for Existence in Our Profession."
Miss M. A. Tupper—"Mistakes and Remedies in Primary Work."
J. A. Sewall—"What Shall We Do With Our Boys?"
Miss S. O'Brien—"The Study of Words."
J. H. Baker—"The Essence of Learning."

After the adoption of resolutions, the following officers were duly elected for the ensuing year:

President, Dr. J. A. Sewall, of Boulder.

Vice-President At Large, Miss Emma Sabin, of Georgetown.

Vice-President, First Judicial District, L. S. Cornell, of Denver.

Vice-President, Second Judicial District, W. A. Donaldson, of Denver.

Vice-President, Third Judicial District, Miss M. A. Pease, of Pueblo.

Vice-President, Fourth Judicial District, Mr. H. Hershberger, of West Las Animas.

Secretary, Miss F. Randall.

First Assistant Secretary, Miss M. A. Tupper, of Colorado Springs.

Second Assistant Secretary, Miss C. Peabody, of Denver.

Treasurer, Hon. J. C. Shattuck, of Denver.

Executive Committee, Mr. F. J. Annis, of Greeley; I. C. Dennett, of Pueblo; Miss N. O. Smith, of Denver.

The Association then adjourned for the session.

FIFTH MEETING.

The fifth session was held at Denver, December 30 and 31, 1879, President J. A. Sewall presiding.

After the President's address and appointment of committees the following programme was carried out:

Mrs. A. A. Aldrich—"Order in the School Room."
L. S. Cornell—"Studies, Ungraded Schools."
A. F. Joab—"Study and the Teacher."
Kate N. Tupper—"School and State."
G. W. Farris—"Cramming Grammar."
Juliette Toll—"Education *vs.* Labor."
Oliver Howard—"Four Years Among the Schools of Weld County."
Miss R. W Bartlett—"Women as Educators."
Ella Leichty—"Language."
David Boyd—"How Far Should the State Educate?"
Aaron Gove—"School Troubles."

The following telegrams were received from other State Associations:

BLOOMINGTON, ILLS., December 30.

Illinois returns the greeting of her mountain sister, and 400 teachers rejoice to find their wandering brothers putting on airs.

A. HARVEY,
President State Association.

MADISON, WIS., December 30.

Greeting acknowledged and returned. May your work be as productive and enduring as your hills.

W. H. BEACH,
Pres. Wis. Teachers' Association.

INDIANAPOLIS, IND., December 31.

From 500 Hoosier schoolmasters to their brethren of the Centennial State, greeting. Shake. By order of Association.

J. L. MERRILL,
President.

Unix.

St. Paul, Minn, December 30.
Our work makes the whole world kin. We send you cordial greeting.

O. Whitman,
Pres. Minn. Educational Association.

The following officers were elected for the next year:
President, J. H. Baker, Denver.
Vice-President at Large, Kate N. Tupper, Colorado Springs.
Vice-President, First Judicial District, T. L. Belham, Golden.
Vice-President, Second Judicial District, David Boyd, Greeley.
Vice-President, Third Judicial District, A. B. Patton, Pueblo.
Vice-President, Fourth Judicial District, H. L. Parker, Colorado Springs.
Secretary, G. W. Faris, Black Hawk.
First Assistant Secretary, Miss B. M. Porter, Georgetown.
Second Assistant Secretary, Miss E. Lichty, Pueblo.
Treasurer, Joseph C. Shattuck, Denver.
Executive Committee, A. E. Chase, Georgetown; Paul Hanus, Boulder; Charles J. Harris, Denver.

The meeting closed with a social entertainment on the evening of the 31st.

SIXTH MEETING

The sixth annual meeting of the Association was held at Denver, December 28 and 29, 1880. The President, James H. Baker, presided, and delivered the annual address. The subject of the address was "The Poetic Principle." From it the following extracts are taken:

"The child, left to itself amidst the natural environments of country life, teaches us true and deep lessons. As soon as by contact with nature through the senses the mind is awakened, he discovers beauty in the flower, is pleased with the green landscape and laughs with Nature's cheerful moods. Before the reason is employed or the intuitions defined, he is attracted by the beauty of natural objects, and is lulled by the soothing influence of music. He soon weaves fanciful pictures in his mental world, builds strange castles, peoples the air with impossible beings, and dreams of wonderful climes. He longs for legend and fairy tale and listens to them with pleased credulity. He chases the butterfly by a natural instinct.

"This tendency of childhood to thrill with the inspirations of Nature, and to love fanciful creations is innate. Were man never burdened with absorbing cares and selfishness this tendency would never leave him. We find here the rudiments of that principle which grows into the ideals, purpose and enthusiasm of manhood, and which controlled by reason moves the world. Happy the man whose childhood has taken thorough lessons in this first school of life.

"Books are but a means to bring us back in later years to a fuller knowledge of Nature's meaning.

"The teacher whose life is aimless and whose labor is mechanical, is not worthy of the calling. Earnestness, progress and love of truth all come from the poetic principle. A nature full of poetry places ideals before the mind and awakens zeal and enthusiasm. The minds of children should be influenced and led by enthusiasts. More of success in life comes from the soul of the teacher than from the routine work. Teaching is sacred, and no one is fit to engage in the work unless he is willing to use all means for right and powerful influence."

The programme was as follows:

Paper—"The Teacher and His Work," W. S. Thomas, Leadville.

Discussion—Aaron Gove, Denver.

Paper—"Development of Faculties in Primary Work," Adele K. Clark, Greeley.

Paper—"Education and the State," E. E. Edwards, Fort Collins.

Discussion—David Boyd, Greeley; J. A. Sewall, Boulder.

Lecture—"The Real Value of Culture," Rev. R. L. Herbert, Denver.

Paper—"Methods of Teaching Elementary Algebra," W. A. Andrus, Canon City.

Discussion—Paul H. Hanus, Boulder; Professor Ira Baker, Georgetown.

Paper—"Education of Women," F. E. Smith, Black Hawk.

Discussion—Charles J. Harris, Denver; Mary J. Thomas, Boulder.

The resolutions printed on a foreging page, concerning the consolidation of the various educational schools in Colorado, were passed after a thorough discussion.

The Committee on Nominations presented the following names as officers for the ensuing year:

President, Isaac Dennett, Boulder.

Vice-President at Large, Miss Mary Thomas, Boulder.

Vice-President First Judicial District, H. M. Hale, Gilpin.

Vice-President Second Judicial District, D. C. Roberts, Arapahoe.

Vice-President Third Judicial District, W. A Andrus, Fremont.

Vice-President Fourth Judicial District, W. C. Thomas, Lake.

Secretary, H. F. Wegener, Arapahoe.

Assistant Secretary, Alice Blackwood, Clear Creek.

Treasurer, Aaron Gove, Arapahoe.

Executive Committee, David Boyd, Weld; F. E. Smith, Gilpin; J. P. Easterly, El Paso.

Mr. Gove moved to amend, by striking out his name for Treasurer, and substituting the name of J. C. Shattuck, the present incumbent. Carried.

The Committee on School Law reported the following:

Resolved, That the granting of State Diplomas be placed in the hands of a committee who will prepare questions for examination for State Diplomas and also for County Boards, and that the Sciences be struck off the Third Class Certificates. This was adopted.

Telegrams were sent to several other states announcing that the Teachers' Institute of the Centennial State was in session.

The Massachusetts State Teachers' Association sent hearty congratulations, and wished all members of the Association a Happy New Year. Ohio also sent greeting.

The meeting closed with a reunion in the evening, which was held at the High School Building, and was well attended. The first part of the evening was devoted to conversation, after which the company was entertained by readings and music.

SEVENTH MEETING.

The seventh meeting was held at Colorado Springs, December 28, 29 and 30, 1881.

The President, I. C. Dennett, delivered the annual address.

The Programme, as printed, was as follows:

Address of Welcome—Rev. T. C. Kirkwood, Colorado Springs.

Response—President I. C. Dennett, Boulder.

Lecture—"Our Foreign Schoolmasters," Prof. Geo. N. Marden, Colorado College.

President's Address—I. C. Dennett, Boulder.

Paper—"Teacher's Work Outside of Text Book," J. S. McClung, Pueblo.

Paper—"Evolution of Primary Methods," Miss Giddings, Colorado Springs.

Paper—"Mathematical Geography," Robert H. Beggs, Denver.

Paper—"Spelling Reform," W. R. Callicotte, Leadville.

Short Addresses:

Lecture—J. A. Sewall, State University.

"Technical Education," Pres. A. E. Hale, School of Mines.

"Discipline of Education," Pres. D. D. Moore, Denver University.

"Social Culture in School," Hon. J. C. Shattuck, Denver.

"Educational Outlook," Hon. L. S. Cornell, State Supt.

Paper—"Cognition in School Work," Robert Casey, Greeley.

Query Box.

Paper—"The Modern School Ma'am," Miss M. R. Campbell, Fort Collins.

Paper—"What to Read and How to Read It," M. J. Spaulding, Nevada.

Interesting discussions on the papers and other topics were participated in by those present.

The report of the Committee on Resolutions, which was adopted, stated that any movement looking toward the adoption of a system of English spelling based upon phonetic principles merits the warmest sympathies and heartiest co-operation of the teachers. It also stated that teachers of acknowledged merit should be relieved from the annoyance of periodical examinations. Thanks were expressed to the citizens of Colorado Springs, especially Superintendent Easterly, for entertainment, to the School Board, to the Executive Committee, to the railroads, hotel, President Dennett, and the daily papers.

The Committee on Nominations presented the following names as officers for the next meeting:

President, J. S. McClung, Pueblo.

Vice-President First Judicial District, Mrs. L. A. Austin, Gilpin.

Vice-President Second Judicial District, P. H. Hawes, Arapahoe.

Vice-President Third Judicial District, A. B. Patton, Pueblo.

Vice-President Fourth Judicial District, C. W. Parkinson, El Paso.

Vice-President Fifth Judicial District, Emma Greer, Lake.

Vice-President Sixth Judicial District, N. A. Andrews, Fremont.

Secretary, Robert H. Beggs, Denver.

Executive Committee, L. S. Cornell, J. W. Barnes, Robert Casey.

Treasurer, Joseph C. Shattuck.

A social meeting was held on the evening of the last day. All enjoyed the music, recitations and refreshments.

The session was a very successful one.

EIGHTH MEETING.

The eighth meeting was held at Pueblo, December 27, 28 and 29, 1882.

The following was the programme:

DECEMBER 27.—7:30 P. M.

Music.
Address of Welcome—Dr. A. Y. Hull, Pueblo.
Response—Aaron Gove, Denver,
Social Reunion.

DECEMBER 28.

Music.
President's Address—J. S. McClung, Pueblo.
"Object Lessons in Primary and Intermediate Departments," Miss Hamer, Trinidad.
"Teaching Literature in Connection with Composition Writing," Miss A. D. Sharp, Gunnison.
Music.
"More Thorough Organization of the Public Schools Essential to the Accomplishment of Their Ultimate Purpose," O. F. Johnson, Maysville.
"Conscience in Public Work," Miss L. S. Tallman, Lake City.
Music.
Lecture, Paul Hanus, Boulder.
Short Addresses:
"What Shall the Schools do for the State," A. B. Copeland, Greeley.
"The Teacher as a Citizen," Samuel Baker, Cañon City

DECEMBER 29.

"Moral Training in Education," Ada E. Bucklin, Cañon City.

"The Teacher's Mission and Duty of Parents," H. B. Coe, Del Norte.

"The Teacher's Preparation," Miss L. K. Noyes, Colorado Springs.

Music.

"Pupil's Fund of General Information," E. C. Stevens, Alamosa.

"Necessity of a High School Course in Our Village Schools," O. J. Bates, Trinidad.

Music.

Short addresses.

"Technical Education," President A. E. Hale, Golden.

"Discipline; Its Relation to the School and State, How Best Secured," Chas. V. Parker, Georgetown.

"Dangers Within the Profession of Teaching," M. D. L. Buell, West Las Animas.

Music.

NINTH MEETING.

The ninth meeting was held at Greeley, December 26, 27 and 28, 1883.

The programme was as follows:

DECEMBER 26—7:30 P. M.

Address of Welcome—A. K. Packard, Greeley.
Response, H. M. Hale—President of the Association.
Social Reunion.

DECEMBER 27.

President's Address—H. M. Hale, Central.
"Exercise in Map Sketching," Hattie E. Hays, Alamosa.

"On Friday Afternoon," Mary E. Whiting, Denver.

"To What Extent Should the Citizen be Educated by the State?" E. Thomas, Boulder.

Discussion—A. C. Courtney, Golden.

Class exercise, illustrating the tonic-sol-fa method, Miss Crabtree, Greeley.

"Does the Prevailing Method of Teaching Modern Languages Produce Satisfactory Results?" F. E. Smith, Greeley.

Discussion—W. C. Thomas, Leadville; T. B. Gault, South Pueblo.

Lecture—Dr. G. De La Matyr, Denver.

DECEMBER 28.

"Should the National Government Give the Cause of Popular Education Pecuniary Aid?" L. S. Cornell, Del Norte.

Discussion—A. D. Bailey, Littleton.

"The Kindergarten and the Public School," Miss Sarah Allen, Fort Collins.

"How Shall We Deal with the Vicious Habits of Reading?" W. W. Remington, Fort Collins.

"The Living Teacher as a Personal Force in Education," Winthrop D. Sheldon, Colorado Springs.

"On the Teaching of English Language," Sarah M. Graham, Denver.

"What Is Industrial Education, and What are Its Possibilities?" President C. L. Ingersoll, Fort Collins.

Discussion—Miss Brown, Black Hawk.

"The Teacher as a Member of Society," Fanny Manly, Georgetown.

The following officers were elected for the ensuing year:

President, David Boyd, Greeley.

Vice-President, W. W. Remington, Fort Collins.

Secretary, W. C. Thomas, Leadville.

Treasurer, J. C. Shattuck, Denver.

Executive Committee, J. C. McClung, Pueblo; R. H. Beggs, Denver; A. C. Courtney, Golden.

TENTH MEETING.

The tenth annual meeting of the Association was held at Denver, December 29, 30 and 31, 1884.

Rev. Myron W. Reed delivered a lecture Monday evening, December 29.

The remainder of the programme was as follows:

President's Address—David Boyd, Greeley.

Paper—"Unmarked Results," Harriet Scott, Pueblo.

"Scientific Temperance Instruction in Schools," A. B. Copeland, Greeley.

"A New Demand," T. B. Gault, South Pueblo.

"Philosophy of Teaching," Miss M. A. B. Witter, North Denver.

"What Lack We Yet?" Jos. C. Shattuck, Denver.

Discussion—Fred. Dick, Trinidad.

Lecture—"The Development of Character," Prof. Edwin C. Hewett, Normal, Ills.

"The Microscope in the School Room," H. F. Wegener, West Denver.

"Method and Variety in School Work," Mary E. Newell, Leadville.

"Theory as Related to Practice in Teaching," Chas. A. McMurry, Denver.

"How to Secure a Judicious Cut-down in Geography," Pres. J. A. Sewall, Boulder.

"Selection and Use of School Libraries," Frona R. Houghan, Denver.

"School Reading," E. C. Stevens, Alamosa.

"Mistakes in School Management," E. L. Byington, Colorado Springs.

Discussion—T. E. Irwin, La Junta.

"The Teacher out of School," Aaron Gove, Denver.

The following are a part of the resolutions passed at the close of this meeting:

Resolved, That the Hon. H. M. Hale, with two others whom he may appoint, shall constitute a committee, the duty of which shall be to prepare and print a pamphlet embodying a history of the schools of Colorado, and especially a history of this Association, now just completing its tenth year of life; and that said committee be hereby empowered to draw on the treasury of this Association to the extent of $200 to defray expenses, said money to be refunded from the proceeds of the sale of said pamphlet.

Resolved, That it is the decided sense of this Association that the true aim of education is the development of character; that the culture of the heart should never be subordinated to that of the head—the training of the conscience to the training of the intellect—and that in the realization of this aim we recognize as the most potent factor a true Christian morality embodied in the character of the living teacher and pervading and guiding all the work of the school.

The following are the officers elected for the coming year:

President, L. S. Cornell, Denver.

Vice-President, ———

Secretary, James H. Van Sickle, North Denver.

Treasurer, Jos. C. Shattuck, Denver.

Executive Committee, George B. Long, Denver; ——— Leonard.

Part III.

Biographical Sketches.

Biographical Sketches.

JAMES H. BAKER.

James H. Baker, for the past ten years Principal of the Denver High School, was born in Harmony, Maine, October 13, 1848; in 1870 he removed to Lewiston, having entered Bates College in that city the year before. His preparatory education was obtained at the Hartland Academy and Nichols Latin School. He graduated in 1873, taking next to the highest rank in a large class, notwithstanding much unavoidable absence. He had a varied experience in teaching in district and grammar schools, in the Topsham Family School for Boys, and as Principal of the Anson and East Lebanon Academies. After graduating from college he was engaged as Principal of the Yarmouth High School. This institution had for many years been known as Yarmouth Academy, but it was at this time converted into a public high school, and its organization and the preparation of a course of study were entrusted to Mr. Baker. The Superintending School Committee of Yarmouth in their report of 1874 speak as follows:

"Mr. Baker has proven himself a good disciplinarian, an excellent scholar and a thorough, systematic teacher. His school has been a model of good order, quietness and hard study."

The following year they say: "The Committee, upon each visit, have found the High School in excellent condition. Its progress has been onward and upward. The method of instruction has been thorough, and the discipline all that could be desired. Indeed, the development of the mental faculties of almost every pupil has been exceedingly gratifying within the past year."

Mr. Baker left this position in 1875 to take charge of the Denver High School. Of his work here the History of Denver, published in 1880, speaks as follows: "The upbuilding of the Denver High School, almost from the beginning, is mainly due to his constant and unwearied efforts. He is a gentleman of ripe scholarship and varied experince in school work. He is a constant student and an enthusiastic teacher, earnestly devoted to his profession. Thorough, concientious and methodical himself, he insists upon the same painstaking care on the part of his pupils. He has labored to maintain a standard of school work fully equal to that of the best similar institutions in the eastern cities. How well he has succeeded the present flourishing condition of the Denver High School will show."

Since the above statement was written this department of the Denver Public Schools has kept pace with the rapid growth of the city, and the development of the school system. The percentage of enrollment in the High School is unusually large. The school is provided with a superior course of study, and in all its departments it is furnished with nearly everything that can contribute to its efficiency. During his residence in Denver Mr. Baker has observed the workings of some of the best High School systems elsewhere and has studied the methods presented in the various departments of the Martha's Vineyard Summer Institute, including a course of lectures in pedagogics. Keeping thus fully abreast with all the most advanced methods of the times he has been quick to adopt their most desirable features, and apply them, with whatever modifications seemed necessary, in his own field of labor.

In addition to his regular work he has been a constant student of several special branches, including metaphysics and literature. He was Alumni Orator at his college in 1883. In 1882 he had a virtual offer of the Presidency of the Colorado State Agricultural College, but decided to remain in his present position. He has been an active member of the State Teachers' Association; he was President of the Association in 1880, and was elected President of the High School and College section for 1885.

AARON GOVE.

Aaron Gove, the Superintendent, has had charge of the Denver city schools since 1874. He was born in Hampton Falls, N. H., September 26, 1839. When he was eight years old he was taken by his parents to Boston, where he passed through the several grades of the public schools. In 1855 his father removed to Illinois and settled in La Salle County, where, for ten years he was the village blacksmith. Mr. Gove began teaching at the age of fifteen, and in the interims between the sessions of his schools completed the course at the Illinois State Normal School. In the summer of 1861 he entered the volunteer service of the United States Army, remaining three years, the last two as Adjutant of the Thirty-Third Illinois Infantry. Soon after leaving the service he returned to his profession and took charge of the schools at his old home at New Rutland, Illinois. In 1868 he accepted an invitation to superintend the schools at Normal, Ill. Here he remained five years teaching, and owning and editing the *Illinois Schoolmaster*, a State educational journal of high standing. In 1874 he was called to the Superintendency of the Denver Schools, which position he accepted, and which he now occupies.

He has devoted his life to the work of the school room. Entering at the age of three years, he has been in the school room almost every school day for forty years. He is a careful and successful manager, a devoted worker in the cause of public education, and in recognition of his superior ability and high standing among the educators of the country, Dartmouth College, at which his eldest son is now (1885) a Sophomore, conferred upon him, in 1878, the degree of Master of Arts.

LEONIDAS S. CORNELL.

Leonidas S. Cornell was born at Athens, Ohio, and at an early age moved with his parents to Fulton County, Illinois. His father was a farmer and found plenty of work for his son for nine months in the year, the other three months being devoted to educational work at the district school. As time passed on the opportunities for attending school increased, and at the age of eighteen Mr. Cornell began teaching, having previously prepared for college at Fulton Seminary. He taught for two years, and then entered the ministry, and took a three-years' course in theology at the same time. Having determined to take a course at college he now entered Westfield College and compled the scientific course and received the degree of B. S. After this he took charge af a congregation at Bloomington, Illinois, which position he held as pastor until failing health caused him to seek a home in Colorado.

He reached Denver in February, 1873, and soon after taught his first school in Colorado, which was an ungraded one in Jefferson County. After teaching two years in this school Mr. Cornell went to Boulder County, and taught until elected County Superintendent of Schools. He was Principal of the Longmont High School when nominated for the office. This office he held for two terms and until the fall of 1880, when he was nominated and elected Superintendent of Public Instruction of the State for a term of two years. At the expiration of his term of office he took charge of the public schools of Del Norte, Colorado, which position he held until the first of January, 1885, when he resigned for the purpose of entering the second time the office of Superintendent of Public Instruction, he having again been elected to that office at the election in November by a flattering majority. At the meeting of the State Teachers' Association, held in Denver, December, 1885, Mr. Cornell was elected President of that body.

In appearance Mr. Cornell is tall and erect, being about six feet two, and weighs 185 pounds. He has dark hair and beard, and a keen grey eye. He is a man of great energy, quick in motion, and capable of doing a large amount of work. Mr. Cornell is now a little past forty and appears to be good yet for many years of useful service in the school work.

LUCINDA WASHBURN.

The subject of this sketch was born in Potsdam, St. Lawrence County, N. Y., in the year 1836, being just a few years too late for that old landmark of pioneer days, the log schoolhouse; and several years too early to reap any special benefit from the State Normal School, now located at that place. The early years of her school life were passed in the district schools of the village and vicinity; while, after that time, the struggle for an education, or rather for the foundation of one, was continued in what was then known as the St. Lawrence Academy, but which in after years gave place to the Normal School above mentioned. Like most children who are born of "poor but respectable parents," she was made to realize early in life the stern but wholesome truth that "Life is real, life is earnest." She was also taught to believe that in order to make that life a comfortable success, it must be filled with useful and pleasant as well as profitable duties. Having developed in childhood a disposition to discipline and govern the household, it was decided by the elder members of the family, as well as by her own inclinations, that she should turn her attention to the art of teaching. As is usual in such cases, there were several terms of what is called "practice work" in the district schools near her home, while she was yet a school girl. This early experience, with the instruction which was gathered from institutes, together with constant study, has enabled her to formulate methods by which she has attained to at least average success in her chosen life work. At the age of 18 she made a trip to Wisconsin for the purpose of visiting friends; also to make an actual beginning in the work of teaching. At the expiration of two years she returned to her old home, where the work was continued in the different districts of her native village, in what was then known as Union Schools throughout the East.

In 1861 she returned to Wisconsin, where she taught for several years in the graded schools of the towns of Ripon and Berlin, the greater part of the time, however, being spent in the former place. Although something of a wanderer, and fond of new scenes and novel experiences, still her deepest, best and warmest emotions were true to her childhood home and friends; and she often found herself wandering back to them, sometimes for only a summer's vacation, at others for a year or two of work and pleasure combined. The Wisconsin work occupied in all about ten years, and was given at three different periods. The greater part of the work done in the East was in her native town; however, two years that were spent in the schools of Watertown, Jefferson County, N. Y., she considers the most useful to herself, as well as in many ways the most beneficial to her pupils, of any of the years of her work.

In 1874 her "Bohemian tendencies" attracted her to the "wilds of Colorado," where she met with cordial words of sympathy and encouragement from active workers who were already in the field and laboring zealously for the cause of education. Her work in Colorado has been confined entirely to the schools of Georgetown and Boulder; that in the latter place being given after the first two years in Georgetown. Her labors in Georgetown began with the opening of the new building and the grading of the schools in the winter of 1875. She is at present finishing her eighth year of service in those schools, where she has worked in each and every department, whenever and wherever in the minds of the people she could best serve the interests of the school. Wherever her future field of labor may be, she feels that the ten years passed in Colorado and in association with her warm-hearted people are to be counted among the happiest of her life, and that she must ever look upon the "Sunny Land" as the land of her adoption, to be returned to from time to time with feelings second only to those which she entertains for her childhood's home.

DAVID BOYD.

David Boyd was born in Antrim County, Ireland, in 1833, of Scotch Presbyterian parents. He immigrated with his father's family to the United States in 1851. The family remained two years in Western New York, when he moved with it to the State of Michigan, where he was engaged in farming until 1857, when he entered the Tecumseh High School with the view of preparing for admission to the Michigan State University. This he entered in the autumn of 1859, having received the Bernard scholarship, one of two then awarded to students who stood highest in the examinations required on entering the classical course of the University.

He remained in the University until the completion of the third course, when he entered as a private in Company I, Eighteenth Michigan Infantry. He remained in this regiment until the autumn of 1863, when he accepted a commission from Andrew Johnson, then military Governor of Tennessee, for the purpose of recruiting negroes for the United States army. In February of next year he was mustered in as Captain of Company A, Fortieth United States C. Infantry, in which capacity he served to the close of the war and was mustered out with the regiment, April 25, 1865.

As he had been pursuing the studies of the senior year during the last year of army life, when he returned to Michigan he was examined with the class of 1866 and graduated as a member of it, then receiving the degree of A. B. Three years later he received from the same University the degree A. M. After graduating he married, purchased a farm in the State of Michigan, where he remained until the spring of 1870, when he joined the colony that settled at Greeley, Weld County, Colo. Since then his principal occupation has been farming, but he has been much connected with the schools of that town and county, having been President of the Greeley School Board and Superintendent of the schools of the county. He has been for some time President of the State Board of Agriculture, the members of which are trustees of the State Agricultural college.

In 1876 he attended the first meeting of the Colorado State Teachers' Association, and has attended and taken an active part in all its sessions since held save one.

Not being himself a teacher, it was no doubt in view of the early and continued interest which he has taken in the Association which led it, at its session held in Greeley, 1883, to elect him its ninth President.

JAMES S. McCLUNG.

James S. McClung was born near **Hennepin**, Putnam County, Ills., July 1, 1838. Until about eighteen years of age he lived on the home farm, attending a district school during the winter terms, generally of three or four months.

In the autumn of 1856 he went to Ohio and spent one year at South Salem Academy, beginning his preparatory work for college.

Returning home at the end of the year, he went to work on the farm again, keeping on with his studies, in part, under the directions of the Rev. John Marquis, a Presbyterian clergyman.

In 1859 he entered the Freshman class at Illinois College and continued there until he completed the Sophomore year. In September, 1861, he took charge of the village graded school at Granville, Putnam County, Ills. At the end of the school year he left his studies and enlisted as a recruit in Company E, Fourth Illinois Cavalry.

In the spring of 1863 he was afflicted with sore eyes, from which he did not recover sufficiently to be able to study for several years. In May, 1865, he was discharged from the service, but found that the condition of his eyes would not allow him to continue his studies at college.

He attempted teaching again in the spring of 1866, at Harvard, Ills., but was obliged to quit on account of his eyes. In 1868 he was appointed to fill a vacancy as County Superintendent of Schools in Putnam County, Ills. In 1869 he was again elected to this office, and at the same time took charge of the graded school at Hennepin, Ills. At the end of the next school year he resigned his office to take charge of the schools at Henry, Marshall County, Ills. After remaining three years at Henry, he resigned to accept a similar position at Delavan, Ills. Here he remained for six years, from 1873 to 1879.

In 1868 he became a member of the Illinois State Teachers' Association, and attended its meetings regularly until he left the State. He was also a member of the Illinois State Society of School Principals; he was Secretary of this Society for two years, and President of the same in the year 1875.

In August, 1870, he was asked to take charge of the schools at Pueblo, Colo. This appointment he accepted, and has just entered on his seventh years' work in this place.

I. C. DENNETT.

I. C. Dennett, the seventh President of the State Teachers' Association, was born December 7, 1849, and is a native of Maine. He was educated in the public schools of Lewiston, Maine, and graduated from Bates College in 1873. For three years he was Principal of the High School at Castine and at Yarmouth. In 1876 he settled in Colorado, first as Principal of Schools at Central City and afterward as Superintendent of Schools at Pueblo.

In 1879 he was elected to the chair of Greek and Latin in the University of Colorado, at Boulder. In 1883 he was transferred to the chair of Latin, which he still occupies.

JOSEPH A. SEWALL.

The State University of Colorado was opened at Boulder on the third of September, 1877, and Dr. Joseph A. Sewall was installed as its first President. Pres. Sewall, when chosen, was Professor of Natural Sciences in the State Normal School of Illinois. He is a native of Scarborough, Me., and received a medical education in Boston, Mass. He afterward pursued a course of study in the Lawrence Scientific School of Harvard University.—*Appleton's Encyclopædia.*

JOSEPH C. SHATTUCK.

was born February 28, 1835, at Marlboro, N. H., and educated in the common schools and in Westminster Seminary, Westminster, Vt. In 1857 he entered Wesleyan University at Middletown, Conn., but soon after went to Missouri to engage in teaching. In 1860 he returned North and taught at Phillipsburg, N. J., and afterward in New Hampshire.

In 1862 he received the appointment of chief clerk in the quartermarter's office at Lebanon, Mo., entering upon its duties January, 1863, and remaining till near the close of the war. In 1866 he resumed teaching in Missouri. In 1870 he joined Union Colony and removed to Colorado, being one of the early settlers of Greeley, and organizing the first graded school in the new town. In 1871 he was elected one of the trustees of the colony, and in 1872 Vice-President, which position he held until he was elected Superintendent of Public Instruction of the State at the first State election, October, 1876. He was re-elected in 1878 and again elected in 1882.

In June, 1885, he was elected by the Trustees of the University of Denver, Dean of the Academic Department, and put in charge of the premises as chief executive officer in all business affairs of the institution. He was married August 17, 1858, to Miss Hattie M. Knight, of Marlborough, N. H., and has three children.

HORACE MORRISON HALE.

was born at Hollis, N. H., March 6, 1833, the fourth son in a a family of five boys and one girl. His father's name was John, and his mother's maiden name Jane Morrison, a lineal descendant of John Morrison, one of the first settlers of Londonderry, N. H., (1720.) His father's ancestors were also early settlers in New Hampshire and Massachusetts. The line of ancestry, on his father's side, leads back to the English, and on his mother's side to the Scotch.

In 1837 his father moved to Rome, N. Y., and, after a residence there of four years, to North Bloomfield, N. Y., where the family remained until the death of the father, in 1852.

His father being a mechanic and inventor, the proprietor of a foundry and machine shop, and also of a manufacturing establishment for agricultural implements, threshing machines, etc., and a firm believer in the doctrine that boys should work, Horace became, at an early age, familiar with tools and quite expert in the various branches of handicraft, both of wood and iron; so that he had the advantages of an industrial education during about nine months of each year, while his schooling covered three months, at the village school.

Soon after the death of his father the family became separated; the older children had become of age, and the younger were thrown upon their own resources. Horace, although entirely without money, resolved to take a college course. In the winter of 1852, the trustees of a neighboring district offered him the situation of teacher of their school, at $14 a month and "board 'round." This he accepted, and thus at the age of nineteen—a mere boy —weighing less than a hundred pounds, taking charge of a country school of forty-five sons and daughters of farmers, was begun a career of public school work that has continued, almost without interruption, until the present time.

In the spring of 1853, with his three months' wages intact, as capital, he entered Genesee Wesleyan Seminary, at Lima, N. Y.; taught another district school the following winter, pursuing at the same time his studies to such an extent that when he returned to Lima, in the spring of 1854, he was upon examination admitted to the Sophomore Class of Genesee College. After completing the Junior year he took a letter of dismissal, and was admitted to the Senior Class of Union College, N. Y., from which he graduated in 1856. He had, by teaching during the winters and by working at mechanical work and in the harvest field during vacations, been enabled to keep up his expenses, and save a little money besides.

After graduating, he taught the Union School at West Bloomfield, N. Y. In the fall of 1857 he went to Nashville, Tenn., and there obtained a position in the public schools; after teaching in a subordinate department one term he was assigned to a principalship, and ultimately the Howard School of 750 pupils was placed in his charge. This position he held until the end of June, 1861. He had the supreme satisfaction of voting twice against the secession of Tennessee, but when the State at the second election decided to go with the Confederacy, he concluded that his usefulness there was at an end.

In 1859, at Nashville, he married Martha Eliza Huntington, his schoolmate of boyhood days in New York, and then an associate teacher.

Leaving Nashville, he, with his wife, returned to their early home, North Bloomfield, N. Y., where was born to them, August 28, 1861, their only child,—Irving,—now Second Lieutenant of Engineers in the United States Army, having graduated at West Point, in June, 1884.

In the fall of 1861, the family moved to Detroit, Mich., and Mr. Hale entered the law office of Hon. C. I. Walker, as a student, where he remained until admitted to the bar in 1863. While pursuing his legal studies he taught an evening school, coached the son of Senator Jacob M. Howard who was fitting for college and taught three hours in the German-English School,— being compelled to do so to keep up expenses, the savings of himself and wife, of previous years, being locked up in Tennessee in real estate and loans, and which for the time were unavailable, having been nominally confiscated as the property of a Union man.

Although admitted to the bar, and ready to practice in all the courts of Michigan, he found that the extra labor undergone had told upon his health. Bronchitis had such a hold upon him that his physician ordered a change of climate and occupation.

In the fall of 1863, leaving his wife and boy at North Bloomfield, he with his brother set out for Colorado, crossing the plains from Atchison to Denver, with a horse and buggy, reaching Central City, his brother's home, in October. During the following four years he dropped intellectual pursuits and sedentary habits, and engaged in out door work of various kinds—mechanical, mining, teaming, etc. In 1865 he returned to New York for his family, crossing the plains both ways with a mule team. This was during the Indian troubles of 1865, and the journey westward covered a period of forty days. Emigrants were not allowed to travel, except with large trains, and picket guards were stationed every night.

The course taken, restored his health completely, and in 1868 he returned to his early love, accepting the principalship of the Central City Public Schools. This he retained until 1873, having in the mean time been elected to the office of County Superintendent of Schools of Gilpin County. In 1873 Governor Elbert appointed him Superintendent of Public Instruction for Colorado, to fill a vacancy, and re-appointed him for two years in 1874. He was continued in this office by Governor Routt, until the admission of Colorado as a State, in 1876. While Superintendent for the Territory, he framed and got through the Legislature, a revised School Law, which has proved to be well adapted to the peculiarities of the wants of the State.

In 1877, he was re-called to the management of the Central City Schools, which position he now (1885) occupies, being his fourteenth year therein, together with the County Superintendency.

At the State election of 1878 he was elected by the Republican party a Regent of the State University for six years. In

1882 he was chosen Mayor of Central City, and again in 1883. Not one of the public offices held by Mr. Hale was sought by him, yet, at one and the same time, was he State Regent, County Superintendent of Schools, City Mayor, and Principal of Public Schools.

Mr. Hale has had the satisfaction of witnessing and contributing to the advancement of the public schools of his State, from almost nothing in 1863, to a rank second to none in the Union. The fates seem to have kept him in the harness, and he has enjoyed the work.

UNIV. OF
CALIFORNIA

Part IV.

State Educational Institutions.

State Educational Institutions.

Of these there are three, the University at Boulder, the Agricultural College at Fort Collins, and the School of Mines, at Golden.

THE UNIVERSITY.

The University of Colorado was incorporated by an act of the Territorial Legislature in 1861, and the location fixed at Boulder. In 1871 three public spirited citizens of Boulder donated fifty-two acres of land adjoining the city, valued at $5,000.

In 1874 the Territorial Legislature appropriated $15,000, and the citizens of Boulder appropriated an equal sum, in cash, for the purpose of erecting à building.

In 1875 Congress set apart and reserved seventy-two sections of the public lands for the support of the State University.

In 1876 the Constitution of Colorado provided that, upon its adoption, the University at Boulder should become an institution of the State, thus entitling it to the lands appropriated by Congress, and further made provision for the management and control of the University, and the first General Assembly of the State made provision for its permanent support by the levy of a tax of one-fifth of a mill annually upon the assessed valuation of the property of the State, and for a fund to be secured by the sale of lands donated by the United States.

The institution was opened September, 1877, with two teachers and forty pupils.

In 1878 the General Assembly appropriated $7,000 for furniture, apparatus, etc.

In the same year Mr. C. G. Buckingham donated $2,000 for a library.

In 1882 the General Assembly appropriated one-fifth of a

mill for additional buildings, apparatus, books, etc., amounting to about $35,000.

The Medical Department was established in 1883.

The first class (six) was graduated in June, 1881, each receiving the degree of A. B.

The present faculty numbers thirteen, and the enrollment shows an attendance of ninety-four.

AGRICULTURAL COLLEGE.

The act creating the Agricultural College passed February, 1877, when the State Board of Agriculture took hold of the enterprise. Fort Collins was the chosen location, and on February 27, 1878, it was voted to erect a building. The corner stone was laid July 29, 1878, and the building completed the same year, but the school was not formally opened until September 1, 1879. The dormitory was erected in 1881, the chemical laboratory in 1882, and thoroughly fitted in May, 1883. A small propagating house was built in 1882 to aid horticulture, while the present conservatory, with curved roof and all modern appliances, was completed September 1, 1883 On the same date the fine mechanic shop was also completed, its machinery in order and ready to run. The College has developed gradually, until there are the following distinct departments, with skilled professors at the head: Agriculture, Horticulture and Botany, Physics and Chemistry, Mathematics, Engineering, and Military Science.

Music has been added more particularly for young ladies.

Of those called to the work of the institution all are present except Dr. E. E. Edwards, first President, Professor F. J. Annis and Professor Elwood Mead, who resigned in 1881, 1882 and 1884 respectively, and are now engaged in other fields of labor.

The College was reorganized on a thorough industrial basis on the accession of the second President, C. L. Ingersoll, when one full line of work was added to the curriculum. Since September, 1, 1882, the growth has been steady and solid, the attendance in 1884-5 being ninety-six, and the graduates in June, 1885, numbering nine.

THE SCHOOL OF MINES.

The State School of Mines of Colorado was established by act of the Legislative Assembly (Territorial) in 1874. In 1879, the (State) General Assembly placed it upon a definite basis by setting apart a fixed tax (one-fifth of a mill) for its support, and in 1880 the south wing of the present building was erected, the faculty increased, and regular courses established; thus enabling the School to insure a competent preparation of its students to fill any department of practical work in chemistry and engineering.

In 1882, the building was greatly enlarged, and can now accommodate over one hundred students in technical courses, containing large lecture and cabinet halls, laboratories, reading room and library; in all, including assay department, over twenty working, recitation, and office rooms. The laboratories and assay rooms are completely fitted for analytical research, and in this, as in all other departments, no appliance is lacking for the prosecution of practical work.

LOCATION.

The institution is situated at Golden, sixteen miles west of Denver, on the Colorado Central railroad, at an elevation of 5,700 feet. No place in the State has a better record for health, and for those acquainted with the climate of Colorado no further recommendation is needed. The mining districts of Clear Creek, Gilpin, and Boulder Counties, are all within three hours' ride by rail.

REQUIREMENTS FOR ADMISSION.

Candidates for admission must be not under seventeen years of age, and be able to sustain a satisfactory examination in English branches, especially higher arithmetic. Those desiring advanced standing upon entrance, will be examined in studies of the course below the class they propose to enter. A certificate from another institution of equal grade as to completion of any required subject, will be accepted in lieu of an examination upon the same.

COURSES OF STUDY.

There are three regular courses of study, viz: Mining Engineering, Civil Engineering, and Metallurgy, each covering a period of four years. During the first and second years the studies are the same for all the courses, after which they diverge into the more technical branches of each specific course.

SUBJECTS TAUGHT.

Chemistry and Assaying are taught chiefly by manipulation in the laboratories, which are the most complete of any in the West.

Surveying includes a large amount of field work, to which certain days are entirely devoted. The use of instruments, plotting and mapping form essential parts of the course.

In the course in Mining Engineering the instruction in the lecture room is supplemented by excursions to various mining and metallurgical works, for which the region offers unusual facilities.

The course in Natural Philosophy is extended to laboratory practice in Photography and Electricity.

Drawing, both free-hand and mechanical, has special rooms and hours devoted to it.

The course in Mathematics is complete; and is continued, the last year of all complete courses, to its application in machines and engineering.

Geology is taught by lectures, amply illustrated by charts and specimens, and by frequent excursions. Few regions afford such a varied field of geological illustration, as the country within a radius of fifteen miles from Golden.

THE STATE INDUSTRIAL SCHOOL.

The State Industrial School is also at Golden. This is a reform school for boys, and was established in 1881. It has been from the first in charge of Mr. W. C. Sampson, and has been very successful in keeping and controlling its boys without high walls, or any prison appliances.

Part V.

Private and Denominational Institutions.

Private and Denominational Institutions.

Of such, founded by the enterprize and liberality of churches and individuals, the State is well supplied. In many of our cities and towns there are small private schools, so transient in character that no record can be obtained.

There are others under the fostering care of various Christian churches which are important factors in the educational facilities of the State. The following sketches of some of these institutions have been prepared, in each case, by some friend of the school.

CATHOLIC SHOOLS.

DENVER.

St. Mary's Academy, founded 1864, boarding institution for young ladies, under the direction of thirty Sisters of Loretto. Gives a thorough education with every accomplishment, and confers diplomas; 75 boarders and 100 select day scholars.

Cathedral Parochial School, under the direction of four Sisters of Loretto; 200 pupils.

St. Elizabeth's Parochial School, under the direction of three Sisters of Loretto; 125 pupils.

Sacred Heart's Parochial School, under the direction of four Sisters of Charity; 250 pupils.

St. Patrick's Parochial School, under the direction of three Sisters of St. Joseph; 125 pupils.

St. Joseph's Parochial School, under the direction of two Sisters of the Good Shepherd, just opened; 40 pupils.

MORRISON.

College of the Sacred Heart, conducted by the Jesuit Fathers; founded September, 1884. A collegiate school for boys.

CENTRAL CITY.

St. Patrick's Parochial School, founded in 1877, under the direction of four Sisters of St. Joseph; 95 pupils.

GEORGETOWN.

Parochial School, under the direction of three Sisters of St. Joseph; 100 pupils.

PUEBLO.

Loretto Academy, founded some ten years ago, conducted by Sisters of Loretto, ten sisters; 90 pupils.

St. Patrick's Parochial School, under the direction of three Sisters of Charity; 145 pupils.

TRINIDAD.

St. Joseph's Academy, founded some ten years ago, under the direction of twelve Sisters of Charity; 200 pupils.

LEADVILLE.

Parochial School, under the direction of seven Sisters of Charity; 500 pupils.

CONEJOS.

Loretto Academy, founded about seven years ago, conducted by five Sisters of Loretto; 100 pupils.

DURANGO.

St. Mary's School, under the direction of three Sisters of Mercy; 50 pupils.

To the foregoing I might add the Institution of the Good Shepherd in this city, who have 135 children under their direction and training; also, the Orphan Asylum, who have 80 children in their institution.

EPISCOPALIAN SCHOOLS.

WOLFE HALL.

is a girls' school under the direction of the Rt. Rev. John F. Spalding, Bishop of Colorado. It was founded in 1867, and is now in its eighteenth year. It occupies the large school building, begun in 1867 and enlarged in 1873 and 1879, situated on Champa street, between Sixteenth and Seventeenth, in the city of Denver. It derives its name from the late Mr. John D. Wolfe, of New York, a generous benefactor, and whose daughter, Miss Catherine D. Wolfe, has, since her father's death, aided the school with a liberal annual gift of money. It had for the year ending in June, 1885, 150 pupils, forty of whom were from outside the city of Denver. They are under the care and instruction of fifteen teachers and a chaplain, all of whom, except the four instructors in music and elocution, are resident in the Hall. French and German are taught by native teachers, and the departments of art and music are systematized into courses of study requiring a series of years for their completion. Besides its large constituency in Denver, its pupils come from all parts of Colorado, from Wyoming, Nebraska, New Mexico, Idaho and Oregon. It has a primary, intermediate and collegiate department. Into the latter no student is admitted without a thorough examination in preparatory studies. The Eclectic Club, a literary organization of the students, publishes the *Wolfe Hall Banner*, a monthly paper containing articles written by the students alone and current events of the school. There is also a missionary organization, the S Agnes Guild. The present Principal is Miss Frances M. Buchan.

JARVIS HALL.

In 1868, Rt. Rev. Geo. M. Randall received a deed of twelve acres of land, near Golden, conditioned on the maintenance thereon of a collegiate school. He at once began the erection of a building with school-room for thirty pupils, alcoves for twenty boarding pupils, and living apartments for the necessary teachers. This building was, unfortunately, blown down on the morning of

Thanksgiving day of the same year. In the following winter Bishop Randall succeeded in securing money enough in the East and from friends in Denver to rebuild. Geo. A. Jarvis of Brooklyn, New York, had given $5,000 towards the original building, and Bishop Randall had named the school, in honor of Abraham Jarvis, one of the earliest bishops of Connecticut, Jarvis Hall. Towards the rebuilding Mr. Jarvis gave an additional $2,000. The School was reopened in September, 1870, and near it was soon after built a building for a School of Mines, with money granted by the Territorial Legislature. In 1872, a third building for a Divinity School was erected with money given by Nathan Matthews, of Boston, Mass. On the fourth and sixth of April, 1878, Matthews and Jarvis Hall were destroyed by fire; and, as the schools in Golden had never met the expectations of their friends, with the approval of their largest benefactors they were removed to Denver.

Since 1879 Jarvis Hall has been carried on at its present site. Year by year its friends have seen changes for the better in its educational management and in its external appearance. In 1885 it was thoroughly rebuilt, much additional room being provided, and the plumbing, heating and ventilating apparatus were completely renewed. The building is now an additional ornament to the city, and the comfort and health of its occupants are as well provided for as in any school building in the town.

CONGREGATIONALIST SCHOOLS.

COLORADO COLLEGE.

The first organized college in Colorado is the memorial of a beautiful American girl, who lost her life for the love of learning. She came as a young consumptive to our Territory in the spring of 1873, and died the next autumn at the age of 14. When visiting General Palmer's residence one day, and looking at the eagles on the rocks and in the air, she suggested the "founding of a school near by, where youth inclined to pulmonary diseases might learn to soar, as light of heart and strong of wing as old Glen Eyre's king of birds," whose life among the cliffs and flight above the clouds symbolized her own aspiring hope and faith, which sang at last,

> "Jesus, lover of my soul,
> Let me to thy bosom fly."

Soon after "Florence Edward's" death her father, Professor T. N. Haskell, laid before the Congregational Conference, at Boulder, her idea of starting a college, open to both sexes and all races, and as their chosen Moderator he convened the Association again in Denver January, 20, 1874, to consider the proposition of several towns in aid of such an enterprise. His address on that occasion was the first pamphlet published in Colorado upon "Collegiate Education" here, though many had spoken and thought of its importance before. The Conference gratefully accepted the offer from Colorado Springs of seventy acres of city land and $10,000 cash, and appointed a Self Perpetuating Board of Trust, which should ever have a majority of Christian men to keep the college evangelical, non-sectarian, and in sympathy with the progress of the age.

The Trustees met at once, named the school Colorado College, and made Professor Haskell its General Agent, to solicit funds and help select a faculty. At his suggestion Rev. Jonathan Edwards, of Massachusetts, was engaged to open (May, 6, 1874) a Preparatory Department, and so many advanced students came that at the end of the first term a committee of educated men passed thirteen of them to the literary and scientific freshman rank. Meanwhile the Agent raised money for a temporary building and endowment pledges of several thousand dollars.

The next year Rev. Mr. Dougherty, nominated by Dr. Sturtevant, of Denver, became the President, and under him, though many of the students were diverted to other colleges and secular pursuits, the work went on.

In 1876 Rev. E. P. Tenny was chosen to preside, aided by several professors from the East. May 31, 1878, he was duly inaugurated. The new stone building, with the library, apparatus and college grounds were formally dedicated. Over 200 annual students were enrolled, and two, Parker Sedgewick Halleck and Frederick Welles Tuckerman, were graduated as "Colorado's first Bachelors of Arts."

The patronage of the College grew, till, in 1884, for monetary mistakes, the Board unanimously voted the Presidency again vacant, which at this writing is still unfilled. The Faculty, Board and students, however, it is believed, were never doing better college work than now. Financial embarrassments have been removed, and ardent, able friends, both old and new, declare that Colorado College must not decline or die. Its founders deem it a memorial almost divine, and the land, deeded for its exclusive educational use, as inalienable and "holy ground."

This denomination also has a school at Trinidad called Tillotson Academy, opened in 1884.

METHODIST SCHOOLS.

Colorado Seminary was chartered by the Territorial Legislature in 1864, and a two-story, four-room building erected on the corner of Arapahoe and Fourteenth streets, in which a school of academic grade was opened in the fall of the same year. Financial embarrassment closed the school at the end of the first year, and the building was ultimately sold for debt. It was bought by Ex-Governor John Evans, and held by him until 1879, when he proposed to donate it to the cause of education if the Board of Trustees would reorganize under the provisions of the act of 1864. This was done. Governor Evans, J. W. Bailey and others made large cash donations, new and commodious buildings were erected, and the property is now valued at $120,000.

In 1880 the University of Denver was organized, and in the fall of that year it began its work in the buildings owned by Colorado Seminary, with Dr. D. H. Moore as Chancellor. Under his direction, supported by an able Faculty, it has had a prosperous career. The Trustees have recently purchased additional property and opened therein a School of Manual Training—the first of its kind west of St. Louis. In November, 1884, Mrs. E. Iliff-Warren offered to endow a theological school as a department of the University with $100,000, if other friends would raise $50,000 to endow other chairs. This having been done, the University may be regarded as having passed its infancy and entered upon its permanent work.

It has a Primary, Preparatory and Collegiate Department. In the latter the standard for graduation is as high as that of any college in the country. Its doors are open to both sexes. It has a boarding department in charge of the Dean of the Faculty and Lady Principal. It provides instruction in music and art.

At South Pueblo the Southern Methodists have established the Collegiate Institute, opened in 1884.

PRESBYTERIAN SCHOOLS.

Under the auspices of the Presbyterian Church a Preparatory School was opened at Salida in 1883, a college at Del Norte in 1884, and another at Longmont in 1885.

MILITARY INSTITUTE.

At Cañon City is located the Military Institute, nominally under the auspices of the Grand Army Posts. It was established in 1881.

www.ingramcontent.com/pod-product-compliance
Lightning Source LLC
Chambersburg PA
CBHW030904170426
43193CB00009BA/733